Wrestling Till
DAWN

Wrestling Till
DAWN

*Awakening
to Life in Times
of Struggle*

Jean M. Blomquist

UPPER
ROOM BOOKS
NASHVILLE

Cover design: Bruce Gore/Gore Studio
Cover photograph: John Sylvester/Westlight
First Printing: March 1994 (5)
ISBN: 0-8358-0697-9
Library of Congress Catalog Card Number: 93-61044

Printed in the United States of America

For Gregory,
    whose love continually reveals the face of God and
    gives my spirit wings,
with deep love

and

For Neil Francis, my fifth-grade teacher,
    who first encouraged me to write, in fullfillment of a
    promise made long ago,
with gratitude

Jacob was left alone; and a man wrestled with him until daybreak. When the man saw that he did not prevail against Jacob, he struck him on the hip socket; and Jacob's hip was put out of joint as he wrestled with him. Then he said, "Let me go, for the day is breaking." But Jacob said, "I will not let you go, unless you bless me." So he said to him, "What is your name?" And he said, "Jacob." Then the man said, "You shall no longer be called Jacob, but Israel, for you have striven with God and with humans, and have prevailed." Then Jacob asked him, "Please tell me your name." But he said, "Why is it that you ask my name?" And there he blessed him. So Jacob called the place Peniel, saying, "For I have seen God face to face, and yet my life is preserved." The sun rose upon him as he passed Penuel, limping because of his hip.

Genesis 32:24-31

CONTENTS

❧

Acknowledgments

The journey from the experiences I share in *Wrestling Till Dawn* to their final written form has been a long one. I am deeply grateful for those who, in many different ways, have journeyed with me.

With a full heart, I thank my husband, Gregory Kepferle, for supporting, encouraging, and loving me beyond measure; Keri Wehlander, dear friend and sister in spirit, for believing in me and for always being with me—even across long distances; John Mogabgab, mentor, colleague, and friend, for drawing out of me what I often don't even know is there; and the late Barb Elliott, good friend and guileless goad, for challenging me to put other work aside in order to finish this book. I also wish to offer warm thanks to the staff of Upper Room Books, especially Lynne Deming and Robin Philpo Pippin, for their skill, grace, and hospitality of heart.

Many other friends, colleagues, and loved ones—too many to be named here—deserve deep thanks. Their encouragement, support, and love have played an indispensable part in making this book possible. I trust you know who you are. This book is a testament to your healing presence in my life.

Thank you and bless you all.

Introduction

How often I've felt like Jacob, wrestling alone in the night—tired, fearful, and confused. Overwhelmed by broken relationships, deep wounds, uncertainty, and failure, dawn seemed a pale, ineffectual hope on a distant horizon. How could God possibly be here, in the midst of such struggle?

My seeking an answer to that question became the seed which grew into this book. Each chapter, like each experience, began as a venture into the unknown. My writing is an attempt at "faith in search of understanding," as Anselm put it. But it is also doubt in search of understanding, because for me faith and doubt frequently go hand in hand. Both, I've learned, can draw us closer to God and deeper into the life of faith.

We all face our own wrestlings and doubts about God's presence in our lives. And though this is a common experience, we often feel alone in our struggles, just as Jacob undoubtedly felt as he wrestled through the night. The world around us and even those people closest to us often avoid, deny, or negate our pain and uncertainty. We are tempted to do the same.

If we refuse to engage our pain, struggle, and uncertainty, we cut ourselves off both from the presence of God within those difficult times and from the possibility of new life emerging from them. By acknowledging our struggles, we embrace all of life and open ourselves to God in every moment.

Struggle is often suspect in our culture and even in our faith communties. Struggle, some feel, reveals only our weakness or lack of faith, our self-hatred or selfishness. But healthy struggle is not masochistic or self-centered. It is a holy encounter where we can grow in wisdom, compassion, and knowledge of God,

13

ourselves, and others. Here we wrestle with the birthing of good: that is what our wrestling is about. Wrestling invites us into a creative encounter that challenges, dares, cajoles, shakes, and draws us into choosing life when it is all too easy to sink into the death of apathy, complacency, powerlessness, indifference, or despair. Struggling that strives toward life is an act of creation. We wrestle through the nothingness of night toward dawn, just as creation once labored forth from the void.

But how can our wrestling become creative? How can it awaken us to life—and to God, ourselves, and others? In wrestling we face our fear. We struggle and strive for healing and blessing, to be touched and named anew. We live in faith that the struggle is not futile or worthless and that we can become more fully human, not less, by facing this challenge. Persevering through hard times does not necessarily mean we will "succeed" as our culture pressures us to do, but it can mean that we will develop an added depth as persons, a greater resiliency in life, a greater capacity for love and compassion, a truer sense of who we really are and of how to care for ourselves and others. Our struggles, instead of defeating us, can help us move more fully and faithfully into life.

The power and poignancy we feel as we read the Genesis account of Jacob's wrestling flow out of its familiarity: we know what it means to wrestle in fear with the power of the unknown. We recognize the rawness, roughness, and reality of struggle. But can we also discern the wonder, and, ironically, the hope intertwined with Jacob's wrestling? Can we recognize the Holy Presence in the dim shadows lurking about our own wrestlings with life?

We all struggle, and there is something hopeful and perversely healing about knowing we are not alone. Stories like Jacob's help sustain and encourage us in difficult times. They remind us that even when we do not recognize that with whom or which we wrestle, God's face may still be revealed to us. When we feel near defeat, Jacob's story reassures us that God is always with us, not only at dawn but in the depths of night as well.

The stories that follow are stories of my struggles with the world around and within me, with experiences of personal challenge and loss, of confusion and pain, of wrestling to see the face of God, of striving to live in faithfulness. In some of these struggles, dawn has broken, brightening the skies of confusion and pain and making my pathway clear. In others, the struggle continues and I trust—sometimes with confidence, sometimes without—that dawn will come. I offer these stories in hope that they may help sustain you in your own wrestling till dawn.

I

⊗

Struggling and Striving

CB

Jacob wrestles desperately, grappling on and on with the one he does not know, straining muscle against muscle, sinew against sinew, through the long hours of the night. Who or what is it that Jacob wrestles with—himself, his fears, his God, or perhaps a confusing mix of them all? Questions race through Jacob's mind as fear clenches his heart: My God, what are you asking of me? Where are you, God? O God, where are you?

Finally the horizon lightens, and Jacob's opponent demands release. But Jacob, though weary and in pain, replies, "I will not let you go, unless you bless me." The unknown one asks his name, then says, "You shall no longer be called Jacob, but Israel, for you have striven with God and with humans, and have prevailed" (Gen. 32:26-28).

Through his struggling and striving, Jacob prevails and receives a new name, which reveals who he truly is: one who has "striven with God and with humans." We often think of "striven with" as "striven against," but another meaning of "Israel," Jacob's new name, is "God strives." Jacob is not alone in his night of anguish, for God is there striving together with him in his confusion, doubts, and fear. Likewise, God strives with us and for us by journeying with us through our pain, offering healing, and drawing us on toward the dawn of fuller life.

Though the circumstances differ, Jacob's questions are my questions as well: What does God ask of me in my struggles, and where is God in the midst of them? Jacob and I both wrestle with broken relationships. We face the reality of past deeds that cannot be undone, while holding hope for reconciliation. Jacob wrestles through his night into a dawning of who he most deeply is, and I wrestle toward a healing that helps me embrace the one God calls me to be.

18

ONE

છ

Of Seeds and Suffering

*T*he pain and brokenness began long before that foggy autumn morning many years ago. I was standing in the kitchen with my foot on a chair, lacing up my shoes for my daily run when my husband walked in. Looking worn and upset, he slumped against the counter. I touched his arm.

"What's wrong?"

"It's just not going to work," he said.

"Are you sure?" I asked, drawing back my hand.

"As sure as I'm going to be."

After months of struggle and anguish, the end of our marriage had finally come, and with it began a journey of faith unlike any I'd ever known.

છ

The early mornings were worst—that time just before the gentle light of dawn eases through the darkness. Those precious moments when I was usually most centered, most creative, most prayerful now became the most painful. I woke trembling, alone in my terror, alone in a darkness that seemed to hold no hope of dawn, alone in the heavy weight of the unknown. At times waves of emotion rolled over me, sobs wracking my body and soul. At other times, I felt stone-cold and detached, as if death had lodged itself in my heart.

Feelings of failure, shame, guilt, and worthlessness tangled together. I felt wounded. I felt abandoned and unwanted. I felt pain as I had never felt before, and, at the same time, I felt nothing.

I wrestled with the meaning of reconciliation. If I were truly a person of faith, shouldn't I be reconciled with my husband? Wouldn't that mean returning to the marriage? If I had faith, wouldn't "all things" be "possible"—even the healing of gaping wounds and deep differences? Wouldn't faith make it possible to forgive and love again? I had once committed myself to working on the relationship, to saving the marriage. Why was I now feeling it was better that it end? Why, on that day I finally slipped my wedding band from my finger, did I feel such relief, such lifting of burden?

Our marriage had withered and died. My life faded like an aging flower, dropping petal by petal to the earth. The challenge of that death was embracing my brokenness as an invitation to wholeness, not defeat. Something deep inside subtly pushed me to seek new life. A slender thread of hope remained. In the turmoil, my faith was stripped of platitudes, easy answers, simplicities. I grappled with the rawness of life. If my faith didn't count here, it wouldn't count anywhere. But I still felt defeated and wearily battled despair. I was challenged to *be* when I felt there was no reason to be, when I felt I was nothing. And I was challenged to pray when I felt I could not pray. Gone was my ability to gather my prayers into a coherent whole. Gone was my ability to think, to center. I cried from the depths of my aching heart. The Spirit groaned with me. Over and over I cried, "Help me, hear me, hold me, heal me."

At times God's presence was palpable, but more often I felt utterly alone. Yet it was when I felt most powerless and most alone that prayer became deeper than words, deeper than understanding. Words cannot express the silent embrace of God. I lost control of my life; I was deeply vulnerable (from Latin *vulnus*, wound), woundable. Ironically, I was also healable. With my defenses gone, God could, perhaps for the first time ever, come fully into my life.

"Tears are a sign of the presence of God," an early Christian writer asserted. Tears I knew well. And in my tears, I came to know the compassionate God. As a child in Sunday school, I'd heard stories of a loving God. Yet many of my experiences of God, interpreted by an authoritarian father, were of judgment and vengeance. Now in my pain, that God of love was touching me and melting away old images from my heart. I didn't quite trust it at first: How could God love me so much to have such compassion? And yet, if God was compassionate, why was I suffering?

In my barrenness, the richness of ritual reassured and sustained me. I hungered for the sacrament of life. Each Eucharist became a plea for healing, a cry for life. My ability to control and shape my life was gone. Ritual, empowered by the Spirit, provided a form to express the formless void I felt within. I could not create new prayers. Singing the psalms and litanies that the faithful had sung for ages gave voice as well as context to my pain. Endless numbers of people had cried out to God in ritual and symbol; now I joined them. Empowered and empowering, ritual and symbol became shorthand script for the steadfast presence of God. During my trauma, tradition and ritual became taproots that helped sustain life.

♋

"I have set before you life and death, blessing and curse; therefore choose life, that you and your descendants may live" (Deut. 30:19*b*, RSV). But how do I choose life, I wondered, when all I feel is death? Yet life with its constant signs of God's loving presence mysteriously surrounded and sustained me. In a letter to friends, I wrote:

In the midst of the grief which produces such soul-wrenching cries at times, I am still able to grasp those small affirmations of life—a beautiful sunset, brilliant red and gold leaves, the soft and warm autumn air. I cling to them as a sign of hope.

These small hints of hope gently nudged a tiny seed from that faded flower of my once-married life. It dropped silently into the rich, dark humus of suffering in preparation for life to come. Even while weighted with death, life subtly stirred within me and I risked choosing life. As a child I'd been taught not to burden others or to share my troubles. Now I realized to continue living that way would be to choose death over life. I joined a new church at this time. I was seeking community and support, but I soon stopped attending. Groups and cliques were set, and I did not feel welcome. I turned to my informal community of faith. Only with the support of friends and loved ones could I survive this terrible time. Awkward and reluctant, still fearing I would be rejected if I revealed my vulnerability and woundedness, I reached out for help. Friends held me when I cried, and they listened for hours as I tried to make sense of the fragments of my life. They offered themselves to me as instruments of healing. They prayed for me and with me. Once, they gathered around me and ritually washed my feet. When I felt unlovable and untouchable, they loved me and touched me, anointing my wounded spirit and binding up my broken heart.

Even with the support of loving friends, choosing life often seemed impossible. The pain and confusion drove me to counseling and spiritual direction, prayer and reading, and countless workshops, retreats, and lectures as I sought healing. The divorce acted as a catalyst of grace that exposed not only the wounds of my broken marriage, but also wounds that had existed since childhood. This strange grace began a healing process I had been seeking for years.

I learned as a child that the greatest possible sin was pride. God, it seemed, did not want me to feel good about myself or the gifts I had been given. Humility was self-effacement and self-denigration. From Teresa of Avila I now learned a new definition of humility: to walk in the truth of who you are. I was challenged not only to embrace my weaknesses, as I was all too eager and able to do, but also to embrace my strengths and gifts. Because I didn't know how to do that, I temporarily entrusted evaluation of myself to a few close friends, my spiritual directors, and a trusted therapist who knew my weaknesses and my strengths. I struggled to honor myself as my friends saw me. By respecting them as bearers of truth, I began to know the Jean they knew—a person closer to my true self.

But even more difficult than acknowledging my friends' perceptions of me was accepting that they *loved* me. Their love challenged me to love myself. Their love revealed the careful interweaving of the love of God, self, and others. I could not fully love others until I loved myself, and love of self and others flows from the love of God. But did God *really* love *me*? I wrestled mightily as I tried to understand what it meant to surrender to God and to God's love. While I was on retreat during this time, my spiritual director shared this saying of a Spanish philosopher: "Heaven [is] when I can love myself as much as God does." Later in the retreat, the pain, anguish, and confusion over the divorce, over how to love and be loved, crashed down on me. Outside a freak California summer thunderstorm mirrored the turmoil inside me. Frantically I tried to understand all that raged inside, and I collapsed on the floor, sobbing. As lightening cracked, I grabbed my journal and wrote,

> God, why? Why? If tears are a sign of your presence, what are you saying to me? *I love you?* How can I believe you love me? How? If I wrestle with this, if I wrestle with you, will you bless me? Oh, God—please bless me, please love me.

At the end of my prayer, as thunder boomed, I suddenly felt drained and calm. The wrestling continued, but slowly I began to feel I was striving *with* God instead of striving *against* God. Although I couldn't fully comprehend it, God loved me.

I grappled repeatedly with the issue of forgiveness. Anger vexed me. Early in life I'd learned to deny anger at all costs. God didn't like angry little girls—only nice, quiet, compliant ones. But now legitimate anger surfaced. One day my spiritual director said, "Why don't you draw your anger?" I returned with a drawing—great swathes of red, blue, yellow, and purple surrounded by thick black. Anger waited for release. Anger and forgiveness were bound together. My growing awareness and certitude of God's love gave me courage to face my anger: God can handle my anger. Why can't I?

I had to recognize and articulate the injustices within the marriage before I could forgive. I had to know, beyond the surface symptoms, what needed to be forgiven. It was very difficult for me to forgive my former husband. Finally I shared my anger with him. Only then did I begin to feel some compassion for him. As I struggled to forgive, I realized that forgiveness was a process, not a simple, one-time act of will. I had to acknowledge my own feelings in order for forgiveness to be authentic. Inextricably tied to the struggle to forgive my former husband was the need to forgive myself. Slowly I grew into that forgiveness as I learned to deal more gently with myself and my imperfections, to acknowledge the parts my former husband and I both played in the failure of our marriage, and to accept that, though marrying had been a mistake, good could still mysteriously emerge from it.

෫

As the months passed, I probed my spirit, my heart, my deepest desires, my pain. I wondered who and what God was calling me to be and do. Honoring and loving myself, being open about my vulnerability, and sharing my pain and anger were difficult and exhausting. A new self, a truer self, was being revealed. Sometimes I longed for my old life simply because it was familiar, not because it was good. Choosing death seemed easier than choosing life, because death was familiar; life was not. I did not move toward life confidently or easily. I stumbled, I fell. Reluctantly I moved on in spite of and because of the pain. Broken and vulnerable, I feared being wounded again. But the possibility of new life—*good*, new life—pushed me on through the night as I clutched close the hope of dawn.

As I embraced my vulnerability, I became stronger. I realized I was a whole person, loved and gifted by God. I didn't have to be in relationship with a man to be complete. I'd known that before, but I hadn't really believed it. Now I knew it was true. I felt a new freedom and confidence in who I was.

The challenges continued. I experienced the healing power of community, but I also experienced its dark side. I don't know their reasons—embarrassment, fear, judgment, uncertainty about what to say or do—but some people cut off contact after the divorce. Others were self-righteous. One woman told me, "My husband and I have had a lot of hard times over the years, but *we* didn't get a divorce." At a workshop I gave on singleness, a participant explained her reasons for coming: "When we got married, my husband and I decided we would never get divorced. I want to know how to help people who are divorced, but I don't understand why they can't carry through on their commitment like we have."

People in destructive or unhealthy marriages—but who, for whatever reasons, could not or would not seek to change their own situations—directed their anger and resentment at me. In this I discovered my own and others' idolatry of marriage. Preserving the human institution was often more important than enabling the divine intent of marriage as an expression of loving, creative, human relationship rooted in divine love. Staying together, or the appearance of doing so, was more important than seeking healing, than choosing life.

These encounters stung deeply and stirred up old feelings of guilt and failure. But they also brought me to a fuller understanding of God's compassion. Through my own pain, I was becoming less rigid, more accepting, more cognizant of others' pain. I understood that their own hidden wounds might be the source of their reactions to me and my divorce. Pain opened my heart and broadened my faith, helping me to accept people for who they were and what they felt. As I became more compassionate, I began, in a very small way, to understand the compassion and love of God. I knew I had been forgiven, and I knew God was present in my struggle and my healing, guiding me toward fullness of life. Although I often wanted to, I could not force that understanding on anyone else. The misunderstandings and judgmentalism hurt, but I was at peace with knowing that choosing life sometimes means moving away from things that ideally should be maintained but which realistically cannot.

⅋

As I became more rooted in my healing and reached out for more of life, I found myself yearning for an intimate relationship with a man. That frightened me. I was afraid that I would enter into another unhealthy relationship, afraid I would be left once again. I was afraid I could not love or trust as I needed to in a committed relationship, and, despite the love of friends and of God, I still feared that I was unlovable. Perhaps I was also afraid I would lose my hard-won sense of wholeness if I was in relationship. Moving beyond the safe love of God and friends required a leap of faith—a risk I wasn't certain I wanted to take. But here the clown God, the God of gracious surprises, playfully offered me a challenging but delightful invitation to love again. So a few years after my divorce, in a totally unexpected way, at a totally unexpected time, a friendship blossomed into a committed, covenantal relationship. Love cast out fear, and I discovered the joy of being in a healthy relationship. Instead of robbing me of my wholeness as I'd feared, the relationship confirmed that wholeness. My new capacity to embrace the wonders and face the challenges of intimacy reflected this. A marriage that is rooted in divine love places love before fear. Trust enables us to move forward in love even when we are afraid—when a conflict arises, when old pain and patterns seep in and disturb us, when we move with cautious, expectant reverence further into the awesome intimacy of life together. Through this, I have come to know more fully the depth of God's love and grace and have learned of my own capacity to love and be loved. I have tasted the nectar of life in the sacramentality of this marriage. I know that God is with us.

But that holy wonder, the mystery of suffering, remains. I do not understand how such suffering could have brought me to the blessings of a truer self and a loving marriage. Did I have to suffer to experience this? Perhaps I could have learned the lessons I've learned about living and loving in another way, but I would not be the person I am today had I not experienced the divorce. Somehow losing myself helped me find my truer self; losing love helped me learn to love more fully and authentically; failing in relationship taught me much about being in relationship in a creative, nurturing way; and experiencing broken trust revealed how precious life is with someone who is worthy of trust. Out of my deepest pain has arisen my greatest joy. ♋

TWO

03

Saying Good-bye, Saying Hello

*I*t is night again. A single fluorescent light casts a strange yellowish-green tinge over the white hospital bed. My mother is dying. Three days and nights have passed since she last knew us—my sisters and brother, my father, myself. We wait for the inevitable end—longing for release and relief, fearing emptiness and loss—unable to believe that we are here watching her die.

We take turns sitting in the pea-green vinyl chairs in her room, tucking our feet out of the narrow aisle as the silent-soled nurses hurry past. We wander the carefully waxed halls and talk softly of things that matter, of things that don't. Earlier in the day Mom hemorrhaged: a small trickle of bright blood seeped from her chapped lips staining the stark white pillow red. We are certain these are her final hours. We wait, lost in that vague vaporous state that engulfs us when reality is so painful that it becomes unreal, surreal. All is starkly etched in my memory—the crisp fold of the sheet, the scraping of the curtain on the rod, the rasp and rattle of her breathing.

Her body turns against her. Her kidneys fail, her lungs fill with fluid, her liver ceases to cleanse the toxins that now slowly poison her. Yet her heart beats strong. Why? Is the life force so powerful that even with body systems battered and broken, surrendering one by one to death, even then it coerces, cajoles: live, live! But does she really live? Her heart still beats, her blood slogs through her weary veins, but her spirit has fled. Her body is simply slow to understand.

It is my turn now to sit with her, watching her body, motionless, except for the erratic rhythm of her breathing. I am tired. I feel helpless—and numb. My thoughts whirl from the present to the past, then forward to the future—then the whirl begins again. What is this life that goes out of her? What will it mean for her and for me? With her death, what becomes of the life we shared?

The green chair is warm now, and all too familiar. She is dying and we will never fully know each other. Only her struggling body remains. Yet her presence is palpable; I feel it keenly. She is in the room, or nearby, but not as I've known her before. I search the dark corners with bleary eyes expecting to see her standing there, but shadows play only upon shadows, dim light upon dim light.

Yet something is here. Or something is coming. I feel it as a maple feels the sap just before it rises in spring, as a rose feels its budding before bursting into scarlet bloom, as a lover feels the call of the beloved before a voice is heard. I rummage through my purse to find a scrap of paper and a dull pencil. Without pausing I write:

> I kiss your spirit
> with my heart
> as memories blossom
> into the living gift
> of you.

This is our final, silent good-bye, for I am not with her when she dies.

○჻

The days that followed were filled with the busyness that accompanies death: phone calls to friends and relatives, arrangements for out-of-town visitors, and preparations for the memorial service. Friends and acquaintances brought food and shared stories of how Mom, with quiet compassion and gentle humor, had touched their lives. She had been important to people in ways we never guessed. The activity-packed days held most of our grief at bay until after the memorial service, when we returned to our familiar, everyday routines. But the familiar wasn't the same. No longer did letters arrive, addressed in Mom's careful handwriting. No more phone calls. No more selecting just the right card for her birthday or Mother's Day.

I kept going because I had to, but grief hounded me no matter what I did or didn't do. Even journaling, which so often helped me work through things, seemed to fail me. I wrote:

> Why is it so hard to write? Is it because so much has happened that I simply don't know where to begin, or because I fear the writing will move me even more deeply into the pain I feel? If I move more deeply into the pain, will I be able to move out of it again? I feel so vulnerable.
>
> Over the past two or three weeks, there has been so little time for reflection, recollection, journaling. I feel disjointed and even desperate not to lose any precious memory of those days, yet it is hard, so hard to write— or to pray. God seems quite distant now, though the presence of God is very real and warm through the caring and concern of so many people.
>
> How do I begin to get a hold of this? Will it help to do a recounting of those days and weeks? Will I remember the insignificant and forget the significant? How can I write of Mom, of who she was and was not, of what she did and did not do, of who she longed to be?

I couldn't think. My mind absorbed nothing. When asked to do something at work, I would quickly forget and have to ask again what I was supposed to do. Tears would come at unexpected times, and not come when I expected them. The world buzzed on around me, but I felt insulated and isolated by my grief.

Although Mom had been growing older and I had known, as all adult children do, that she would someday die, I still was caught off guard by her death. There is no way to fully prepare for the death of a parent. There is no way to fathom the immensity of the ties, the interconnectedness of lives. And, very bluntly, a parent's death faces one with one's own mortality. No longer was I part of the "next generation"; with my mother's death I became part of the "older generation."

After her death, I realized anew how little I knew about her. She was a quiet, introverted person, who kept most of her thoughts and feelings locked carefully and safely inside. Part of my grief was for the parts of her I'd never known and now would never know—and also for the parts of me that she would never know. We were not close as mothers and daughters sometimes are. Her death left me struggling not only with grief but also with questions about us. Could our relationship have been different? Could we have been other than who we were and who we were able to be in those thirty-three years of shared life? I'd known her as a daughter, but what didn't I know of her? As a child, as an adolescent, as an adult, what did she expect, or hope, or dream her life would be? What unexpected joys and sorrows did life bring?

⁰⁄ₛ

My grandparents emigrated from Denmark with Mom's older brothers and sister shortly before the beginning of the Great War. Mom was born in Iowa, the only native-born American in her family. She was proud to be Danish, but proud also to be American. She readily embraced the notion that the United States was a kind and generous benefactor to the rest of the world, a notion that sometimes blinded her to its shortcomings.

Though she came from a home where Danish was spoken, she had little patience with immigrants who did not learn English or adopt "American" ways. Ironically, she often spoke harshly and contemptuously of immigrants, though hers was not a blanket prejudice: the immigrants she knew well were all exceptions, not like the "others." Her attitude puzzled me for a long time because she was an intelligent, sensitive, and compassionate woman. She was capable of empathizing in other situations, and she usually recognized the complexities of life. Why not here? Because I believed that compassion expressed more accurately what lay at her heart, I began to realize that her contempt for immigrants hid a deep personal wound. Her own feelings of inadequacy, self-doubt, and perhaps even self-hatred overwhelmed her compassion at times. To bolster her sagging sense of self-worth, she did as we all do from time to time: she found someone she could put down, someone she could be "better" than. Her prejudice was a desperate but crippled attempt to be human, to feel good about herself.

That part of my mother, which struggled so desperately to establish and maintain a sense of self-worth, lives on in me. I've battled feelings of disgust and even hatred of myself. At the same time, as is often the case with those who struggle for a basic sense of self-worth, I've teeter-tottered unrealistically between feeling better, then feeling worse than others. Because my self-expectations were so high, I projected those on others, and no one, including me, met my standards. I've often felt alone in the world, and I suspect that Mom often did too.

ೞ

Her parents were artisans: her father, who was a master cabinetmaker, also crafted musical instruments; her mother was a seamstress. They loved to garden, and their home and yard were filled with flowers. Even during the cold winters of northern Iowa where they settled, flowers bloomed brightly inside while snow covered the ground outside. Each December Mom spoke of her mother's Christmas cactus, carefully placed in the darkness of the cellar at just the right time and brought out weeks later to bloom profusely for the holidays. Grandma always counted the bright pink blossoms, sometimes numbering two hundred or more. Then, as they withered and faded, she pinched them off. Though Mom loved plants and they flourished with her care, she never grew a Christmas cactus, at least that I know of. Now I wonder why.

When Mom was nine, her father died unexpectedly and her family split up in order to survive. By the time she was eleven, Mom was working as a live-in family helper, as well as going to school. What were those years like for her? "What were the families like that you worked for?" we asked. "Some were good; others were not," she'd respond tersely. Her childhood shattered by her father's death, she sought security, stability, and love. And when she gave up on love, she continued to strive for security and stability. Financial security was never really hers. I remember her—outwardly strong and stubborn and inwardly, I suspect, in pain—wearing a single, faded blue paisley housedress so there would be money for our school clothes. She sometimes sacrificed future possibilities at the altar of stability to keep her world from falling apart again. I've done the same.

She was bright—one of her favorite high school classes was physics—and talented musically. She sang a solid alto and played the piano well after having only a little instruction. What did she dream of doing? Without money or other support, college or vocational training were impossible. Did the saying "you can do anything if you really want to" weigh on her, making her feel like a failure? What was it like not to be able to use her intellect, her talents? She married, had four children, and worked through the years as egg gatherer, cleaning woman, bookkeeper, postal clerk—none of which fully tapped her intellectual gifts or artistic talents. There was a dearth of intimacy as well—in her marriage and in her friendships. I know of no one with whom she fully shared herself.

She read, even though she had little time for it. In her later years, she turned frequently to escape literature—romances and mysteries. She avoided movies and TV programs that did not have happy endings. "There is," she said, "enough tragedy in the world already."

As she aged, bitterness with life crept in, but she was such a private person that perhaps the change was only apparent to those closest to her. It hurt to see her bitterness grow, to sense the pain it reflected. But I rarely heard her speak of her own private world: her broken dreams, frustrations, angers, disappointments. The bitterness protected her from further hurt, but it blocked her from hope and healing as well.

○ß

She rarely hugged or kissed us, other than a perfunctory good-bye kiss as we left for school each morning. Yet she showed concern and affection in other ways. When I was little, she cut my peanut-butter-and-jellied toast diagonally (not horizontally), because that was the way I liked it. When I was sick and wanted one of our cats to keep me company in bed, Mom would look inside and out till she found one and then she would bring it to me. The touch of her work-roughened hand on my forehead, when I had a fever or was in pain, calmed and comforted me.

One Halloween she sewed late into the night making witch costumes for my sister Carol and me. I was deeply disappointed for us and for her when they didn't win the costume contest at our grammar school. Another Halloween, she arranged to get off work (which she rarely did) so she could attend my class party. Before the party, she mixed, baked, and frosted chocolate cupcakes, then carefully decorated them with whimsical faces of marshmallows, chocolate chips, candied corn, and other goodies. She packed them carefully, so they wouldn't be damaged en route to the school.

Upon arrival, she offered them to the room mother, who quickly set them among the store-bought cookies, packaged-mix cupcakes, and paper cups of apple cider. The room mother then resumed her conversation with the other mothers, leaving Mom standing alone. All much younger than she, they barely acknowledged her. Their lives were so different from hers: they were full-time homemakers with nice clothes and homes; she worked on a ranch, living in a small house provided by the owner, and she wore older clothes. Mom smiled at me as she leaned against the low counter near the back of the room. When refreshment time came, my classmates dashed to the counter. Mom watched as delighted children devoured her cupcakes, but she remained alone. When the party ended, we drove back to the ranch together.

Each December, although weary from gathering thousands of ice-cold eggs as well maintaining our home, she baked dozens of rich, carefully shaped Danish Christmas cookies late at night after we children were in bed. She hid the fragile cookies in foil-lined boxes or a big clear glass cookie jar at the back of her bedroom closet. But we knew where to find them. One by one, we'd sneak to the closet, quietly open a box or the jar, and pop a cookie or two in our mouth. We were never punished for eating the cookies, though Mom warned sternly, "There won't be any left for Christmas"—but there always were.

I often saw her uncertainty, her perfectionism, her feelings of inadequacy. When I was in grammar school, I would bring home permission slips to be signed for school outings. They always asked parents to print their child's name, but Mom had never learned how to print. When she was in school only cursive writing had been taught, and she was always self-conscious about her efforts, even though her writing was thoroughly legible.

Almost anything she undertook, she did well—yet for her it was never done well enough. When she was complimented on a beautifully sewn dress, she pointed out all its flaws. When someone said how wonderful her lemon meringue pie was, she'd reply, "Well, the meringue is a little 'weepy'" or "The crust isn't quite right." The flowers she raised never grew as brightly or profusely as they could have. Though people liked her, she always felt somehow on the periphery, that she didn't belong. She lived as an outsider, economically and socially. Over the years, I began to understand how my own perfectionism and dissatisfaction with myself and my work, at least in part, had become so deeply ingrained. If Mom, who did things so well, considered her work flawed, what did that say about mine?

☙

She did so much, and yet there were still times when I longed for her to be more than she seemed able to be, times when I also longed to be more than I could be. When I was in fifth grade, I checked out a book on the "facts of life" from our one-room town library. Mom saw it and asked me if I'd read it. "Most of it," I replied cautiously, though I had in fact devoured the entire book. "Well, then you know everything you need to know." I said nothing, a bit embarrassed I suppose, but wishing that I'd lied and told her that I hadn't read it. Inside I cried, "But I want *you* to tell me about it!" Just as we never discussed hopes and dreams, successes or failures, neither did we discuss sexuality, love, or intimacy. What pain did she have around these, and what pain did she unwittingly pass on?

Many years later when I was thirty and my first marriage failed, I went home to try to explain to my parents what had happened; I hardly understood it myself. Since we'd never talked about the important things in our lives, sharing was difficult. Relieved when our awkward conversation ended, I escaped to the bedroom and began undressing for bed. A moment later someone knocked lightly on the door. When I opened it, I found Mom standing there. "Sometimes," she said haltingly, "parents wish they could go through things so their children didn't have to." Then she quietly closed the door and walked away. She'd said much more than she had ever said before, and yet I wished we could have talked more. I longed for her to be more than who she could be at that moment. I wanted her to hold me and comfort me, to let me know she loved me, to assure me I was lovable. Yet

I too was unable to reach beyond who I was to risk a deeper encounter or possible rejection. Like characters in a Bergman film, we came so excruciatingly close to the final vulnerability that could blossom into intimacy, only to be kept apart by an invisible wall of fear. But the risk she took to say those words still moves me. She cared deeply and communicated that in the only way she could, a way that must have taken great effort and courage—a way that she could have just as easily let pass by.

☙

I don't remember her ever saying, "I love you." The only time I remember saying "I love you" to her was in the hospital that August afternoon as she lay dying. How hard and awkward it was to speak words that had never been spoken before. I didn't know what to say, and she could hardly speak. Her words twisted around in her mind and her mouth: a sentence began with one thought and finished with another. Piecing together the fragments to decipher what she was thinking, feeling, and saying was like putting together a stubborn jig-saw puzzle, and I never had liked puzzles. I fought tears. Proud, controlled Mom, now so uncontrolled, trying finally to say what was in her heart but hardly able to do so. I leaned over the bed rail, lay my head on her shoulder, and held onto her—something I hadn't done since I was a child. She hugged me with what little strength she had left. "I love you, Mom," I said. Her words slurred, but she spoke this time in whole sentences: "You're a good gal, a good girl. You all were good kids. Take care of each other." Her response nearly broke my heart. I longed to hear her say, "I love you." Perhaps she had once hoped to speak those words, but the time for that had passed. I felt sad and empty. I loved her still, but, I wondered, did she love me?

I felt so inadequate being with her in her dying. What could I say, what could I do other than be there? How could I respond when she struggled to say, "I'm scared"? My stomach tightened. I took her hand and mumbled, "We'll be right here," knowing we couldn't be there, not in her dying. I often remember her fear, wondering what I could have said or done that would have helped. What would have comforted her? Could anything? What did I know about dying?

She was a person of deep but quiet faith, a faith that had seen her through many difficult times. She lived her faith rather than talked about it. Her honesty as she neared death was raw and real. For once she didn't try to cover up her feelings, and her faith was apparent in that. Why, I wondered later, do we so often assume that when we are scared, we lack faith? Perhaps a greater lack of faith comes when we refuse to acknowledge our fear. Are we afraid that God can't handle our fear, that somehow God will reject us if we falter? Faith, like courage, has something to do with going on *in spite of*, in spite of unbelief or fear. It means going on in the face of uncertainty. It means going on even when we don't know how to go on. Mom, I think, knew in-spite-of faith well. It carried her through a challenging, often difficult, and sometimes empty life.

ℭ℈

Several years have passed since my mother died. I've wrestled with her mothering and my daughtering, remembering the many times we fell short of intimacy. I've been poked and prodded, haunted and hurt by the what-ifs, the if-onlys, and the should-haves. But I now realize that sometimes, no matter how hard we try, who we are is not enough to bring healing and wholeness to another, even one we love very much. Time and grace have slowly and gently moved me toward acceptance of who I was as her daughter and who she was as my mother. Acceptance, I've found, is an active, dynamic process, and only acceptance that is "lived into" or "wrestled into" allows our grieving to turn into growing.

I regret not knowing my mother as I would have liked to have known her, and perhaps she regretted not knowing me as she would have liked. But one of the extraordinary things about us humans is that for all we know, there is always much more that could be known. Not everything we'd like in this life is possible, yet grace can speak even through the failures, the disappointments, the bereavements, the attempts at loving and wholeness that somehow fall short of their mark. Reconciliation can occur, understanding can deepen, acceptance can grow even after death separates us.

My mother's death was not only a good-bye to life; for me it was also a hello to life, a challenge to see that life encompasses death, not vice versa. Her gentle legacy—sensitivity to the Spirit, respect for the mind as well as the human spirit, compassion for animals, a love of beauty, a respect for fine craftsmanship, a delight in good humor, a sense of endurance, a commitment to doing a job well no matter what it is—invite me into fuller life. Her struggles with perfectionism, self-acceptance, alienation, loneliness, excessive self-reliance do the same. The Spirit of Life invites me to move through the struggles toward healing and to learn that the healing I experience and claim touches the lives of those whose lives touch mine—past, present, and future. In some small way, my mother is healed as I am healed, because she is a part of me and I am a part of her.

Each day my mother's life touches mine, and I continue to learn from her and of her. Our relationship did not end with her death. It simply continues in a new way, revealing places for growing, for reaching beyond, for striving toward the fullness of life and the presence of God that she sought and that I seek as well. ❧

THREE

❧

Out of the Valley of Desolation

Y ou're no good and you never will be!"

Harsh, taunting, seething with contempt, the voice cut to my core. But I could not escape it, because the voice was my own.

I don't know when I began talking to myself like that, but I suspect I was quite young. I grew up with that ever-contemptuous, ever-damning internal voice. A less than perfect score on a test could evoke, "You're a failure. You can't do anything." Knocking a towel off a rack or a paper off a desk would earn a barbed internal retort, "You are such a klutz." And when I felt lonely and unwanted, perhaps the most damaging voice of all sneered, "No one could ever love you."

Never would I have dreamed of talking to another person like this, yet I attacked myself continually. To defend myself, I developed a compulsion for perfection. For years I tried desperately to prove my worth through achievement. Throughout my school years I pushed myself in academics and in extracurricular activities: sports, band, clubs. I served on committee after committee and in office after office. I was yearbook editor, junior class president, student body president; I was even chosen queen of my hometown's annual festival. But in the midst of all this, I felt worthless and depressed.

I remember the pain I felt one day when I saw a high school classmate slumped against a tree. When I asked what was wrong, he said, "My mom doesn't like anything I do. She always talks about all the stuff you do. She wishes I were like you." I didn't know what to say. Inside I ached. Why would anyone want their child to be like me? His mother could only see me on the outside. She had no way of knowing the pain I experienced inside, because, exactly as her own son did, I felt I wasn't acceptable for who I was. Despite an outward appearance of confidence and accomplishment, inside I continually battled feelings of being nothing, of being a fake, of being unlovable.

In college the drive to achieve continued: student government, music, academics—all on top of working to fill the gap between college expenses and scholarship resources. But it still did not ease my depression, my feeling of worthlessness. Once when I was invited to attend a banquet for faculty, top students, and guest scholars, I nearly turned the invitation down because I didn't feel I belonged there. Only after much urging by the campus pastor did I go.

On the evening of the banquet, I dressed slowly, my body weighted down with my feelings of worthlessness. Two of my roommates were also going, and they talked excitedly as they dressed in their best clothes, something rarely seen on our informal campus. If nothing else, they laughed, the evening would be a welcome respite from cafeteria food. As we drove to the banquet, I sat in silence in the back seat. Inside I kept hearing, "You shouldn't be going. You're not a scholar. You don't belong there." The evening was painful and confusing, but I forced my tears back and pasted a stiff smile on my face. All around me people were talking, laughing, enjoying themselves, but I felt as if I were tightly sealed in a glass box. Life went on around me, but colors were muted and people were distant. Nothing could touch or penetrate the hard case that confined me. Other students, some of whom were not as good students as I, were proud of being there; they felt they deserved to be there. Why couldn't I feel the same way? Why couldn't I feel good about or satisfied with anything I ever did?

After dinner, the lights dimmed in preparation for the keynote speaker. In the darkness, I lost the battle with my tears, though I managed to keep them to a trickle that could be subtly and silently wiped away. What a relief when the evening was finally over and I could return to the dorm and cry, but quietly, so my roommates wouldn't hear.

The compulsion to achieve continued after I graduated from college and began working. *If only*, I thought, if only I could get the right position, if only I could achieve something really important professionally, I would finally feel OK about myself. *If only*.

But achievement was not the answer. My striving was futile. Other people may have been impressed, but I was not. I felt empty. Over the years I had become an expert at discounting positive comments, compliments, and accomplishments, and equally adept at exaggerating the negative. The net result was an ever-growing self-contempt and a deepening depression from which I could not escape. Nothing filled the void inside. Nothing, not even success, could silence the internal taunts and condemnations. Nothing could allay the nearly constant depression. I prayed for help, as I had for years, but God didn't seem to hear.

Most of the time I suffered "low-grade" depression. Ever present and energy sapping, it nonetheless did not prevent me from functioning. Ironically, my strong and over-developed sense of responsibility, as well as my fear of having others discover the "true" me (who I was certain they would reject), usually kept me functioning even at the worst of times. But the people around me had no way of knowing the harangues in my head, the great effort it often took to get out of bed in the morning, the emptiness, the void, the frequent despair. They could not know the times I wrapped the sheets and blankets tight around me, feeling incredibly heavy and weary of life. They did not know the times I slept to escape, to cope, to recuperate from the depression that drained me physically, emotionally, and spiritually. They did not know the times I slept wanting never to wake up.

Yet life went on around me and often I was caught up in it. As hard as those years sometimes were, they still held moments of laughter, friendship, fun, and wonder at the beauty of the world. Without my knowing it, those moments helped build a foundation for healing that would come many years later. But even on the good days, the threatening gray cloud of depression was never far away.

CB

I carried the millstone of depression with me into my first marriage. The depression was impossible to hide in the intimacy of marriage, and the problems that emerged in our relationship only accentuated it. My feeling of being unlovable, only briefly and superficially allayed by marriage, grew even stronger when that marriage failed. I felt I had given so much and tried so hard, and yet the relationship crumbled and I was left behind. I failed even at love. Never had I experienced such pain, confusion, or bewilderment. And never could I have imagined that this agonizing time would hasten the healing of my deep, pervading sense of worthlessness.

The divorce marked a time of both spiritual aridity and spiritual ferment, the latter of which I can see only in retrospect. The pain drove me deeper into despair than I had ever been driven before. The divorce forced the shadowy, unspoken, unarticulated pains of my life to the surface where they could finally be identified and encountered. Somehow, by confronting the pain and despair directly, I began to uncover some of the deeper, long-abiding pains in my life.

The divorce forced me to act. I wrote feverishly, filling journal after journal as I probed my heart and spirit. I read about divorce, about suffering, about finding meaning in life, about anything that might help me understand what was happening to me. I prayed in anguish and confusion, reading and reciting the psalms that echoed my own despair. I asked, if it were possible, that this cup be removed from me. I cried silently as Jesus had once cried aloud, "My God, my God, why have you forsaken me?"

I sought spiritual direction and guidance, and I sought counseling. Marya, my therapist, was skilled, compassionate, and patient—but not too patient. She listened, supported, encouraged, affirmed, and pushed me when I needed pushing. Her deep understanding and sensitivity to the spiritual as well as the emotional dimensions of my struggles kept me on track. She did not let me forget, even in despair, that the Spirit was present and healing was possible. I doubt she ever said that directly, but her own spiritual composure and certitude spoke eloquently, even in silence.

After we had been working together for some time, exploring issues related to the divorce and those that extended beyond it, she paused one afternoon and said, "I think you've been depressed since you were a child, but you have developed an amazing ability to cover it up." I did cover my depression well, because I'd learned as a child that many, if not most, feelings were not acceptable to those around me. And with a child's understanding, I interpreted that to mean, because I had those unacceptable feelings, *I* too was unacceptable. I feared letting anyone know what I really felt, because I sensed that would be dangerous. In that fear, I developed various ways of coping—including a ready smile, a compliant spirit, and an independent manner—that disguised my feelings and my depression. Eventually, in my adeptness at covering up, I hid my true feelings even from myself.

After years of successfully hiding my depression and of fearing that people would find out about it, I felt strangely relieved when Marya said she believed I had been depressed since childhood. That rang true, and it helped me make sense of some of my life that had seemed senseless. I wasn't just fabricating this whole thing; it had been with me a very long time, and I was only beginning to work my way out of it.

Yet I don't think I consciously believed I could move out of my depression fully. It had been with me so long that I couldn't imagine life without it. Yet somehow, perhaps only by grace, the healing process had begun. But even though I desperately wanted to be freed of the burden of depression, I also feared healing. I feared change. The depression was bad, but it was familiar. What if I moved out of the depression I knew so well into something worse? Who would I be? Would I lose the meager sense of self that I had struggled to establish? Depression had been a way of numbing myself against harder realities which, particularly as a child, I had no way of challenging, rectifying, or escaping. Depression allowed me to cope. But now, as an adult, the ways of coping I learned as a child were stifling me. Could I learn to live another way?

☓

When Marya encouraged me, "Act as if you aren't depressed—act as if you have options and confidence," I would grit my teeth in protest or shake my head in bewilderment. To "act as if" seemed to require that I be someone other than myself. "If you do that, you really will be a fake," my internal accuser whispered. But somehow the Spirit cracked the wall of my resistance just enough for me to see that this "acting as if" was a way of choosing life instead of death. The deadness I had experienced for so long was not what God wanted for me or for anyone.

Marya's encouragement to "act as if" was a concrete way of loosening the constricting bonds of depression and death, and of introducing me slowly and gently to life. As I tasted more of life, the "acting as if" would drop away and I would begin to fully live each and every moment. The "acting as if" was itself an act of faith, a movement toward healing and life. In one sense an act of faith is always an "acting as if." It is a choosing of faith in spite of doubt, goodness in spite of evil, life in spite of death. And in the choosing of faith, good, and life, they became reality.

Learning to choose life was, in a most practical and pragmatic way, a leap of faith that affirmed the presence and reality of God in the midst of my most prolonged life struggle. It meant telling the truth about myself to myself. It meant acknowledging and accepting compliments and affirmations. It meant embracing the wonders of creation even when I felt distant and removed from everything and everyone around me. It meant many things, but most of all it meant doing things that I often thought I simply could not do.

My most difficult leap of faith was acting as if I liked myself—and "liking" it had to be, because I couldn't even conceive of loving myself. Choosing life meant acknowledging myself as a person of value and worth. It meant finding my true self, for at the heart of my depression was a lost self longing to be found. Ironically, my acting "as if" became a way of finding, revealing, and releasing my true self, a self I didn't even know. The only way I could climb out of the valley of depression was by walking in the truth of who I was, which meant owning my feelings, gifts, and limitations, and embracing myself with holy reverence as one created by God.

For years I'd felt I had something innately wrong with me, and if that could just be fixed or eliminated, I'd be OK. This led to a strange preoccupation with myself as I struggled to find a way to "fix" myself. I don't think I was "self-centered," as depressed people are often accused of being, as much as I was seeking to center my self, to find a center point of safety and balance where I could stabilize and grow healthy. As I struggled to find that center, I discovered that I must tackle two intertwined tasks, one psychological and one spiritual. Psychologically I needed to develop a "realistic concept of self," which included recognizing, understanding, and accepting myself as a person with talents, limitations, and innate worth. In short, I needed to accept myself as a human being with all the positive and negative traits that go along with being human. Spiritually I needed to develop a "gracious sense of self," an attitude of reverence and thanksgiving for the gift of life—and very specifically, the gift of *my* life, of *me*.

The intersection of these two tasks created tremendous conflict. I had grown up believing that anything that had to do with "self" was wrong. "Good Christians" always put themselves last, not first, in everything from the line in the school cafeteria to the line at the Pearly Gates. Because pride was the cardinal sin, I put myself down so I would never be guilty of being prideful. And since pride was such a terrible sin, I received no encouragement to develop my gifts—ironically the very gifts given me by the God I was supposed to be honoring by being "humble." Somehow the whole understanding of self that was presented to me as "Christian" was skewed—self-negating, self-deprecatory, self-destructive. The "Christian" ideals of "self-negation" and "self-denial," instead of being freely chosen movements of the heart by mature people of faith, were used inappropriately as child-rearing practices. Anything that reflected the self was to be denied; anything that spoke of the heart's desires and longings was to be negated—this was "God's will." In actuality, these "Christian" ideals more frequently justified the un-Christian assertion of power over the powerless: children, women, certain social and ethnic groups. I could not begin to make progress on the psychological task of accepting myself until I had resolved these spiritual issues.

Fortunately I had been exposed to something other than the self-negating, self-denying form of Christianity. I had also learned of a loving God, though that loving God never seemed as vivid as the vindictive one. Then one day I read a familiar Bible story. I had read it and heard it many times before, but this time I truly *heard* it for the first time. The Pharisees are confronting Jesus, hoping to trap him in a theological error that will discredit him (Matt. 22:34-40). The Pharisees ask: "Teacher, which is the great commandment in the law?" And Jesus answers, "You shall love the Lord your God with all your heart, and with all your soul, and with all your mind. This is the great and first commandment. And a second is like it, You shall love your neighbor as yourself" (vv. 36, 37-39, RSV). I, of course, knew I was to love God and my neighbor, but for the first time I also heard that I was to "love my neighbor *as myself.*" If I didn't love myself well, I couldn't love my neighbor well either. This verse haunted and heartened me, and eventually it became the key that allowed me to escape the dungeon of destructive spirituality that had negated and nearly destroyed me.

The very foundation of faith, Jesus said, involves loving God, loving self, and loving others. For me, loving self incorporated both the psychological aspect of recognizing, understanding, and accepting myself as a complex human being, and the spiritual aspect of gracious "selfness" in which I could reverence and give thanks for the gift of my life, for the unique person known as Jean Marie Blomquist. Reverencing and giving thanks meant being most fully the person I was at heart, at the very core of my being, and developing and using the unique gifts God had given me.

○§

Moving toward healing was a way of choosing life, and it involved all of me—body, mind, spirit, and emotions. I couldn't simply "will" myself to like me. I couldn't tell myself that my depression wasn't rational, because that would not have helped. It made no difference whether the depression was rational or not. Whatever it was or wasn't, it existed and permeated my whole life. I needed a concrete place to begin, and that beginning place was my negative thoughts and self-condemnations.

I began to listen carefully, to observe how often and how negatively I spoke to myself. Then with great reluctance and doubt that it really could make any difference, I began talking back. At first I felt very silly, but talking back was no sillier than talking negatively in the first place! When I wrote an article, arranged some flowers, or baked a cake, and then harassed myself for it not being perfect, I would say in my new voice, "You did fine. Maybe it could be better, but that will just take some practice. Be gentle with yourself." If I knocked something down and said, "You klutz!" I would immediately counter that with "Just pick it up; it's no big deal." Each negative thought would be countered, defused, and replaced with internal encouragement and more accurate assessments. Sometimes I grew weary of being watchful and the old voice drowned out the new. Often I didn't believe myself. I remained convinced for quite some time that I was a failure and that I was unlovable. Just talking in a new way didn't magically make things better, but at least it started moving me in the right direction. Talking back wasn't easy, and at times I would become so exasperated with myself that I would blurt out, "Just get off your own back!" But slowly I began to listen to myself: maybe I wasn't so bad after all.

Acting as if I liked myself also involved learning to accept my own feelings. But before I could accept them, I had to learn what they were. My feelings were murky and mired together in what I called "being down." It is difficult to explain how I began consciously and unconsciously to sort them out, but I do know that part of the process was physical. I didn't feel very good about my body, which didn't fit the image of "perfection" promoted by television, movies, and the advertising world. Despite being strong and healthy most of my life, I lived an uneasy truce with my body. It was, I felt, like everything else about me: inadequate. So it came as a surprise when my body played a significant part in my healing.

In the midst of my divorce, I received an unexpected invitation to join a newly forming liturgical dance group. I had no formal dance training, but I had always wanted to study dance and this gave me the opportunity to do that. I worked out, rehearsed, and performed with the group. I also studied dance for a while at a local dance studio. The more I danced, the more I learned about my body. And, although I had always been physically active in one form or another, I now discovered the challenge and the release of expressing emotions through bodily movement. The more I moved physically, the more I sensed the Spirit literally moving within me. I became aware of subtle and not-so-subtle muscular changes in my body and the messages they conveyed. Very slowly I began to sense my feelings physically, even before I comprehended them cognitively or affectively.

About three years after I started dancing, I was sitting in one of my favorite places for reflection, a community rose garden in the hills above my home. My mother had died recently. I was still deep in grief and, I thought, depression. But as I sat on that warm wooden bench looking out over San Francisco Bay, I realized I didn't *feel* the same physically as I did when I was depressed. When I was depressed, I felt an overall heaviness, an overwhelming oppressiveness, a deadness, a disconnectedness from everything around me. What I was feeling now was a heaviness, yes, but it was more concentrated or focused, especially in my chest and solar plexus. I felt not so much disconnected as out of sync. These little physical clues were a revelation. I wasn't depressed; I was sad and grieving.

I began to watch for physical clues to other feelings and emotions. I discovered, for instance, that when I felt manipulated, my stomach muscles would knot themselves into a hard fist. But the one emotion that eluded physical definition the longest was anger. It continues to be the most difficult feeling for me to recognize, but slowly and with practice I am becoming more adept at recognizing and feeling my feelings at the time I actually experience them.

Learning to feel my feelings was a slow and sometimes agonizing process. It also confused and discouraged me, because the more healing I experienced, the more I could literally *feel* my feelings. As I felt more, my numbness, which had once insulated and protected me, began to fade, allowing the jagged edges of my fresh feelings to stab and cut my fragile new self. But as sharp as the pain was at times, it was also a sign of healing, a concrete testimony to my moving out of death toward life. As I abandoned the gray chamber of depression, I encountered the colorful spectrum of life in all its vividness and vitality. This spectrum included a wide range of feelings and emotions, some of which, such as joy and happiness, I quickly embraced as part of my life. But it also included others, such as anger, envy, disgust, and hate, that I was more reluctant to accept as a part of me. These were the "negative" feelings that had been most unacceptable when I was a child. To embrace all of life, I had to acknowledge even these difficult and sometimes frightening feelings. To shut them out would only invite the pall of depression to cover me once again. To do that would be to choose death over life, and I was determined to choose life.

⌘

My journey out of long-term depression followed a slow and tortuous route. Yet each step, however small or unsteady, became the foundation for the next step. Facing the depression itself was the only way out of that deep valley.

The journey was often a lonely one, yet I was never alone. Even in the depths of my depression and often without my being aware of it, God was present and the Spirit nudged me insistently toward healing through unexpected avenues such as divorce, dance, and "acting as if." The Spirit also moved through friends and loved ones who, even when they did not know my anguish, loved and cared for me. And, perhaps most exquisitely and simply, the Spirit moved through the wonders of creation, through animals and wild places and delicate flowers, whose beauty and solace alone could silence that destructive inner voice. As I began to experience some healing, as I began to open up to the possibility of my own worth and acceptability, I could finally receive this diverse gathering of wonder and love into the foundation of my own life. These building blocks, which once had seemed so far removed from me, began to gather together with the fragile stones of my fledgling self-identity. They strengthened me in my weakness and supported me in ways both seen and unseen.

Like Jacob's limp, my wrestling with depression continues to stay with me in many ways. Because of depression I have not lived and loved as fully as I could have. I have lost personal and professional opportunities. One of the challenges I have faced in moving out of depression is grieving and accepting (although often reluctantly) those losses. Yet, although these losses are real,

I also know I have gained a measure of wisdom, sensitivity, compassion, and maturity in the process. I still am challenged not to get stuck in the "if onlys," as I remember what might have been. The temptation toward that can be very strong. Hope, confidence, and trust atrophied during my depression and had to be exercised—slowly, gently, and carefully at first—in order for them to grow strong. I must continue to exercise them each day.

I still sometimes ache for those things—the affirmation, acceptance, and assurance—that might have kept depression from getting such a strong hold on me when I was a child, but my early wounds are no longer open and gaping. What remains are the scars, and scar tissue is strong. Healing has not come in the way I expected, but it has come nonetheless. There are no quick fixes for depression, but there are small steps, and each step must be celebrated and affirmed, for it is the foundation of the next step, the foundation of healing itself. And as healing begins, more healing comes.

I still fear depression, though I rarely wrestle with it as intensely as I did before. When I begin to feel down and that "downness" lasts a little longer than I am comfortable with, I often fear that once again I will be dragged down into that deep valley of desolation. But healing has brought resiliency, and I have learned that, though the fear is real, the healing is also real. To face depression and seek healing is an act of the heart, an en-Spirited heart that knows an intimate way to its own healing. For when we live most deeply in our own hearts, we also live in the very heart of God. ଔ

II

୯ଓ

Fearing and Facing

After years of exile, Jacob is going home. His wives and slaves busy themselves with preparations for the journey. Giggling children chase one another around tents and bundled belongings, while sheep bleat and donkeys bray. Silent oxen paw at the dry ground and slowly munch on their fodder, as camels, bored with the whole affair, stare off into the distance.

Jacob wanders aimlessly around the camp. He wonders, have twenty years eased Esau's anger? Can Esau ever forgive me for cheating him out of his birthright and blessing? He wanted to kill me then; he swore he would. Now God wants me to go back home, back to Esau. What do I face—reconciliation or death?

Suddenly a shout rings through the warm afternoon air. Jacob jerks his head toward the sound. Everyone looks up, even the camels. The children abandon their games and run to the edge of the camp. The sheep and donkeys are still. Here come the messengers! The ones sent ahead to find favor with Esau have returned. Though hot, tired, and dirty from their journey, they breathlessly deliver their news: "We came to your brother Esau, and he is coming to meet you." Jacob's shoulders relax. He smiles.

But then they continue, "and four hundred men are with him" (Gen. 32:6). Jacob's smile freezes; his gut churns. Then he shouts: "Divide the flocks, the herds, the camels into two companies." The herdsmen scurry to obey. "You people," flailing his arms through the air, "go with that company," and whirling around to another group, he shouts, "And you go with the other." Jacob clutches his queasy stomach as he reasons, "If Esau comes to the one company and destroys it, then the company that is left will escape" (v. 8).

Then Jacob prays. Desperately he reminds God of an earlier promise: "Return to your country and to your kindred, and I will do you good" (v. 9b). "Deliver me, please," Jacob pleads, "for I am afraid ..."

(v. 11). Then, swallowing hard, he continues: "Yet you have said, 'I will surely do you good, and make your offspring as the sand of the sea . . .'" (v. 12). His prayer ends and his heart pounds. One question nags him: Can I trust God's promise?

Jacob has good reason not to trust. When he left home, Esau wanted to kill him, and his last twenty years with his Uncle Laban have been one experience of broken trust after another. That night Jacob wrestles desperately, trying to make sense of his life. As dawn nears, the wrestling ends in an extraordinary way. The one with whom Jacob wrestles gives him a new name and a blessing. Grasped by a wonder he can't comprehend, Jacob somehow knows that in his wrestling he has encountered the Holy. He names the place of his struggle Peniel, "the face of God." "For," Jacob says, "I have seen God face to face. . . " (v. 30b). As the sun rises, he limps away. Both strengthened and vulnerable, he prepares to meet Esau.

In the wrestling, God draws Jacob out of the past, into the present, and toward the future—toward healing, life, and hope. It is here that Jacob sees the face of God. Jacob's fear is transformed; it no longer paralyzes him. Now he knows God is with him as he faces what—and whom—he must face. Great uncertainty remains. Undoubtedly fear remains as well. Jacob still must face Esau and his four hundred men, but he does so, in spite of his fear and in spite of his limp.

In the stories that follow, I fear and I face. I move slowly toward deeper trust and faith as I lean on God, let go in spite of my fear, and leap (or limp) into the unknown.

FOUR

CԷ

To Touch the Fringe of God's Garment

I t began with what I thought was the flu, but it would not go away. My doctor, after lab tests returned negative, stated that I had a "virus of unknown origin." The only thing I could do was rest and eventually I would feel better.

But the "unknown virus" dragged on for weeks and months. I forced myself to go to work, napping on my lunch hour and on breaks whenever possible. My "free" time basically became time to maintain survival: groceries, laundry, banking. In the evenings and on weekends, I was so exhausted that I did only what I had to do.

I grew more and more discouraged. I prayed. I cried in frustration and fear, for somehow I sensed something beyond a "virus" was attacking my body. I went to another doctor and was told to take a vacation. I did, but it did little good. Friends and acquaintances offered advice: "Quit your job," "Take this vitamin," "Change your attitude," "Try this diet." Some, reflecting the shadow side of the holistic health orientation, asked, "What haven't you worked through?" implying that illness always reflects psychological or emotional disturbance, while health reflects physical, spiritual, and emotional balance and harmony. Those asking this question, of course, were physically healthy. Job's friends, I quickly learned, are still alive and well today.

I dreaded having people ask me how I was, because I was so tired of saying, "Not very well." Eventually most stopped asking; they didn't like hearing continual bad news. They also probably wondered if perhaps it weren't "all in my head," since the doctors couldn't find anything wrong. I wondered myself if that might not be the case. Maybe I was simply going crazy.

Eventually I did quit my job. I began to feel somewhat better. The episodes of illness shortened and occurred less frequently. I married. I wrote. Doors were opening. I felt happier than I'd ever felt before. Personal and professional challenges, of course, continued, but life was good and getting better.

Then the episodes of exhaustion, nausea, headaches, joint pain, and fever became more frequent and severe. One bout dragged on and on, with the worst symptoms I had ever experienced. My body was so weak that even the short walk to our mail box left me panting and exhausted. Joint pain or severe headaches often kept me awake during the night. Nausea was nearly constant. Discouraged and scared, I wondered: Do I have something terrible? Am I going to die?

I returned to my doctor, but a complete physical revealed nothing. Test results were normal. Then I read an article on frequently misdiagnosed diseases. Many of the symptoms of lupus[1] matched my own. My doctor didn't think there was sufficient evidence to support a lupus diagnosis, but she ran additional tests anyway, probably more to allay my fears than anything else. A few days later, while I was fixing dinner, the doctor called. "There are," she said, "some abnormalities in the lupus test." I wrote in my journal:

> Greg had come home while I was on the phone. I motioned for him to go out and stir the soup. When I got off the phone, he asked me who I'd been talking to. I said the doctor and then haltingly told him what she'd said. He held me as I cried a little, then we continued

fixing dinner. When we sat down and said grace, I started crying again as I looked across at Greg, who had such love shining in his face. I don't want to be separated from his love. Why, when things began to feel like they were beginning to go better in my life, did this have to happen?

The next morning I reflected on this life-changing news in my journal. I wrote about my prayer time earlier that morning and how the only prayer I could articulate was,

"I'm going to need help." As I meditated, the image of a beautiful shy wolf came to me. Perhaps I need to embrace this wolf (lupus). Given how I've hated myself and hated my body all my life, I'm not surprised that this is an autoimmune disease. All the hatred has been taken into the body itself. I feel angry about that—that I learned to hate myself instead of love myself. If I'd been truly loved and affirmed as a child, I wonder, would I have this now? Perhaps. Perhaps not.

A few days later the lupus diagnosis was confirmed. I was frightened, angry, and relieved all at once. I had *known* something was going on in my body—finally there was proof of that. For four years, doctors had brushed off my symptoms as "just a virus," "stress," or "psychosomatic" in a way that had frustrated me and made me doubt my own knowledge of my body. I was vindicated, but that vindication was bittersweet. Now I faced the possibility, the probability, of lifelong illness.

Life would go on, but within the limitations set by the lupus, and I'd never dealt well with my limitations. Would I ever be able to backpack again, to enjoy the solitude and wonder of less-traveled ways? Would I be able to hike with my husband to the bottom of the Grand Canyon, or even take a walk around the neighborhood after dinner? What about children, travel, work? How much of life would be off-limits because I was chronically ill? What toll would the illness take on our young marriage? There were so many questions and very few answers, yet . . .

> In the midst of the bewilderment, the anger, the fear, there is a sense of the adventure of entering the unknown. Perhaps I'm entering a time of accelerated growth. I fear falling back into the clutches of depression. I fear hating myself because of the illness. I fear, I fear, but I go on—in what? in faith? in hope? I don't know. But somehow, in some crazy way, this is part of life too. Can I embrace even this?

As days passed, I wrestled with the reality of being chronically ill—sometimes believing it, other times thinking it couldn't be. Then came the monotony of living with illness each day.

> Yesterday I felt dull and dry, almost numb spiritually. Words, concepts, scripture seemed empty. There is a passion that goes with desperation, a feeling of life and vitality in the midst of the turmoil and fear. That passion seems to fade when one realizes, when *I* realize I'm in this for the long haul. The future spreads out, vast and unknowable. What do I do now? How do I begin to piece the quilt of my life back together with the addition of this unexpected and odd-shaped piece called lupus? I need to keep reminding myself this is part of life too.
>
> The other day as I walked to the post office, so weary that the two-block venture seemed nearly impossible, I watched people—pushing strollers, crossing the street, getting off the bus—and thought, why can't I just have a simple, ordinary life? And then I realized no one does, or that everyone does, including me. The challenges of life do not present themselves to only a few, although at times it seems some people do get more than their

share. Everyone has a unique set of challenges, trials, joys. Rarely, when we really think about it, would we trade our sorrows for another's, if we could do that. I think of the Hasidic story about the tree where people hang their sorrows. Everyone then circles the tree with the freedom to choose any other person's sorrows. Each always chooses again his or her own. Maybe in a rather perverse way that shows we love ourselves—we'd rather be ourselves than anyone else.

But even if I really wanted to be myself—and I sometimes questioned that—I still didn't want to be sick. What, I began to wonder, does "healing" mean? Is remission "healing"? Are "healing" and "cure" synonymous? What about all those stories about Jesus healing people? Could that happen to me?

I became almost reckless in my openness toward God, which included seeing and seeking God and God's movement and presence in places and ways I perhaps otherwise would have ignored or avoided. I explored a range of resources on healing—some mundane, some exotic. I devoured literature on healing, traditional and nontraditional. I even read about lupus, but I found that I didn't want to learn about illness; I wanted to learn about *healing*.

Advent—the season of hope, the season of waiting, of anticipation. My hope is for healing—and I am waiting. I find it hard to anticipate healing. I guess I anticipate the worst. There are at least two parts of me—the one ready to give in, to despair, to accept that the worst will be what comes; and the one ready to fight, to say I'm going to beat this, I'm going to get well. The two continually wrestle with each other, alternating which has more power. . . .

My prayer for the past several months has been that I might move more deeply into the Spirit. Is this illness the answer, or an answer, to that prayer? Is that the way God works? If so, I don't like it. Or does God work *even* here? I don't know. Sometimes I feel so confused. We think we know so much about God and the ways of God, but sometimes I wonder if we know anything at all. Does what we know or don't know make any difference?

As I struggled with my faith and its relation to the lupus, my desire for healing kept me probing possibilities and potentialities. Could faith heal me?

Since there is no medical cure for lupus, I am turning to spiritual healing, to prayer. I feel like such a neophyte. There's a part of me that feels a real sense of trust and certitude in the healing power of prayer. Another part of me is really doubtful. . . .

Even if prayer might eventually bring healing, at the moment I had to learn to cope with illness on a daily basis. Certainly I'd been sick before, but I always knew I would get better. The lupus was different. As the days and weeks wore on, a slowly rising panic began to take hold of me: I couldn't remember what it was like to feel "normal," to feel "well." I now faced the loss of something so basic, something so close that I hardly knew it was there: wellness, "normalcy," my heretofore daily experience of reality. The lupus permeated every aspect of my life—eating, sleeping, playing, praying, loving, and especially working.

The apartment needed to be cleaned, I needed to shower and wash my hair, and I had to prepare for the interview. It was crazy to push so hard, but I wanted and needed to. When I got out of the shower and looked in the mirror, the red butterfly rash was glowing on my face, brighter and heavier than ever before. From deep inside "I hate you!" erupted. My real anger at

having lupus surfaced. I feel angry that it keeps me
from doing things like this—just basic work.

As ordinary routines and responsibilities slipped from my
hands, I sought ways to make my life livable. An article sent by a
friend gave insight into this new experience of living: "When one
is ill the illness becomes one's work. When we ask a patient how
he feels we are asking him to talk about his work."[2] Friends
dealing with chronic illness were invaluable. Together we could
talk matter-of-factly about our "work" without fears of being
labeled "complainers" or "catastrophizers."

I struggled to maintain some sense of self-worth and to
salvage a sliver of self-esteem when nearly everything I once had
done now seemed impossible. A wise friend wrote, "Please
remember that the lupus doesn't define *you*." Though inextricably
intertwined, the threads of identity and illness, I had to learn, are
separate.

Slowly I became more aware of the ebb and flow of my
energy. I learned that certain environments and people were
healing and helpful for me; others were not. I felt guilty,
unloving, "un-Christian" when I avoided being with certain
people when I was ill, but the drive for life and healing reminded
me that I could not be all things to all people. And I gave thanks
for those who did bring healing.

I just want Greg near. His presence is healing for me.
So is his love. That's where much of my hope resides—
in the power of his love, in the power of our love. Our
love is at least somewhat tangible, although it often is
still incomprehensible. If our love has such power, what
can the power of the love of God be like? Our love is
part of God's love. I think that's another one of my
basic questions: What does it mean to be loved by God?
Shouldn't I know the answer to these questions by
now?

The many questions about living with illness, seeking healing, and understanding the love of God continued to hound me. Answers were few and far between, but I kept seeking.

What should I be doing to seek healing? Should I be "doing" anything? Do I kid myself by thinking I can "do" something? Should I be in spiritual direction? Should I be having massage, bodywork, acupuncture, acupressure? It takes energy just to pursue the possibilities, and sometimes I simply don't have the energy. Where does that leave me? I pray. I pray that my body may live in harmony with itself. I give thanks for the healing already taking place. I pray that God will surround each of my cells with a golden, healing, protective circle of light, a light that will make it clear to my antibodies that these cells are friends, not foes. I pray that my antibodies will be encircled with silver, that they may become what they are to become—the protectors of my body. I visualize the light encircling my other cells, the silver encircling my antibodies—what a wonderful illuminated dance my body makes! . . . God, dance with me—in my heart, in my body, in my life. Be my heart, my body, my life.

In this whole process of seeking healing, how do I find the balance between doing and being? How do I know when to fight and when to let go? When does fighting, when does seeking, become control? When does letting go become passivity or apathy, or worse—despair? What is surrender? What is grace? Aren't I to use what God has given me—my intellect, my resourcefulness, my curiosity, my desire for healing and wholeness? But how and when do those get in the way? Bernie Siegel writes that healing is hard work.[3] It is. But isn't it also no work at all, because in reality we don't heal ourselves? We can encourage it, help create an environment for it, but we can't do it. Yet we are an indispensable part of the process. This is all very confusing. I don't know how to make sense of it at all. I don't understand. Perhaps this is where faith comes in. It carries me through that which I don't understand. It also assures me that even if I don't "do" the "right" thing or that if I "am" not in the "right" way—if I am not "being" as I should, whatever that is—healing is still possible. That is grace. Yet I can't help but believe that somehow seeking or striving counts for something. For what, I don't know, but I do believe it matters.

ଓ

In many ways, surrender is at the heart of my pursuit of healing. That should, I suppose, be no surprise since surrender is such an integral part of faith. Some people would undoubtedly say I should simply "surrender to the will of God" and then I wouldn't have to struggle so much. But I don't think it's that easy. Surrender is not an abandonment of ourselves in the face of difficulty, nor is surrender synonymous with submission. We yield ourselves to God freely, not under coercion. Surrender is not resignation. It is an invitation into something greater, fuller than ourselves. It is also an invitation to be ourselves more fully.

Surrender is not so much a giving up as it is an *opening* up. It is a dynamic living and striving in the face of the unknown. When we surrender in faith, we enter into the power of God, into the realm of all possibility. We open ourselves to new perspectives, thoughts, and dimensions of life and living yet to be explored. We do not give ourselves up in the sense of extinguishing ourselves, but instead the little lick of light we are joins with the holy flaming that is God. We are brought more fully into ourselves and at the same time brought into that fullness which is greater than all that is.

What does surrender mean for me in relation to my illness? It means connecting my story with that of the woman who, yearning for healing, dared to reach through the crowd to touch the hem of Jesus' garment (Mark 5:24*b*-34). My surrendering to the power of God involves a reaching, a yearning for what is beyond, just as that woman on that dusty road in Palestine stretched out her trembling hand to touch the fringe of Jesus' garment. She reached in spite of the crowd, in spite of the people and circumstances that blocked her access to the power of healing. She reached in spite of the religious and cultural taboos designed to restrain her. She reached in spite of her weariness from twelve long years of illness and of being an outcast. This brave woman's faith is revealed not only in her final reaching for the hem of Jesus' garment but also in all her previous reachings, yearnings, wrestlings to seek wholeness. She reached in many different ways—and I reach too.

The lupus is with me each day, whether I feel sick or well. I continue to hope, seek, and pray for healing, drawing on all the resources God gives me. I do not know if I will ever be healed, but I still seek healing with my whole being—body, mind, and spirit. Both because I believe healing is possible and because in my weakness I fear that it is not, I pray as I reach out each day, "I believe, help my unbelief." ⍩

FIVE

CϬ

Money Problems

My husband, Greg, and I drove uneasily onto the Bay Bridge that crisp, dark January evening. Our uneasiness was due not only to crossing the bridge for the first time since a section had collapsed in a major earthquake—repairs had only recently been completed—but also because of our destination.

We were on our way to a church in San Francisco for the first session of a series called "Bringing Money Out of the Closet." The flyer we'd received had sparked our interest, because our attitudes and feelings about money were primarily negative: fear, guilt, avoidance, defensiveness, and, at times, envy, self-righteousness, or even greed. We knew these were not healthy attitudes spiritually, psychologically, or practically, and we hoped participating in the money series would help us find a way out of our pecuniary quagmire.

A mixed group gathered at the church: a disabled woman living on a fixed income, several professionals, a venture capitalist, sales people, human services workers—some single, some married, some with families. Our commonality was our struggle with money. After introductions, we sat quietly answering a questionnaire. "Do you have enough money?" it asked. I hesitated. Although Greg and I had moved beyond our leanest times and now had adequate income to meet basic expenses and still have some left over, I resisted answering yes.

For much of my life money had been scarce. Money, it seemed, had always been a "problem," and I had a hard time seeing it or imagining it as anything other than that. Perhaps I was afraid to say I had enough, almost as if what I had might disappear if I acknowledged its existence. Or maybe I felt guilty or sinful, because there were so many people who had so much less than I did. I am not quite certain what all my feelings were, but they were many.

"How will you know when you have enough money?" the next question asked, piercing to the heart of the matter. It wasn't, at least after a certain point of basic subsistence, a matter of how much money I had, as much as how I related to it. I knew, of course, of the need for a right relationship with God. But what might it mean to have a right relationship with money?

Stimulated by the questionnaire, the group began to share stories, feelings, and long-forgotten memories. I sat quietly at first, noting uncomfortably that most people came from much wealthier backgrounds than my own. Old doubts and questions quickly surfaced: How could they have problems with money? How could they understand what it means not to have money? How could they understand the fear of scarcity, the feelings of immobility and lack of options that few resources had set deep within me?

But the longer I listened, the more I discovered how similar our feelings and experiences were. Stereotypes began to crumble. One person, whose father was a physician, talked of growing up feeling that "the wolf was at the door," despite their relative affluence. Another said that talking about money at home was a greater taboo than talking about sex. Heads nodded in agreement. For some, money meant fear: one person followed her family's custom of spending money as quickly as it was in hand, because it might not be there tomorrow; another responded to fear by being excessively tight-fisted, saving so diligently for a rainy day that generosity and spontaneity were stifled. One woman breathed a sigh of relief as she confessed that she was paid too much, while another wrestled with what to do with money inherited from a relative.

I had always thought that I struggled with money because it had been so hard to come by. But now I saw that many, maybe most, people struggle with money, regardless of their financial circumstances. Clearly, despite its abundance or lack, money is a big, and often troubling, issue.

Money is not simply a medium of exchange or means of payment. It has become a measure of value, not only of goods or services to be bought or sold, but also of our very selves. In our society, with its strong emphasis on material acquisition and monetary accomplishment, it is difficult not to equate our money with our selves. We say, quite honestly perhaps, that money can't buy everything, but still feel great tension and ambiguity over the fact that there is much in this world that money *can* buy. And, although we would rather not admit it, we would often like to have a bit more of the power, freedom, and autonomy that money often gives.

I have wrestled with money frequently over the years, and I still find it difficult to admit the confusion and tension it sometimes reveals in my life: the deep feelings of inadequacy, the longing for stability and security, the anguish that what I do is not valued, the desire for material goods, the fear of being unable to survive financially. Somehow as a person of faith, I feel I should not have these problems and questions, these fears and desires, and yet I do. Why? Why does money cause such anxiety? Is there some healthier way of responding to and dealing with money? Can I somehow learn to deal with money in faith rather than in fear?

❧

I grew up in a working class family. For most of my youth, my father and mother were ranch workers. We—my parents, two sisters, one brother, and I—lived on the ranch in a two-bedroom house provided by the ranch owner. In addition to managing our household, my mother gathered the eggs of the ranch's 35,000 chickens. My father fed and otherwise tended the chickens: cleaning the chicken houses, providing rudimentary veterinary care, and maintaining the buildings. He also irrigated, disked, and sprayed the surrounding almond and walnut orchards, as well as doing or supervising whatever work the ranch required.

Like my siblings (and our parents before us), I began working while I was still a child. My first job was gathering eggs, a monotonous and dirty task that was hot in the summer and cold in the winter. Once in a while the monotony was eased by a garter snake twined in an egg tray, an injured chicken that needed assistance, or a very occasional (and sometimes disastrous) dash to the egg house with a loaded egg cart—a race with my sister to see who could finish first and go in for the day. When I turned twelve, I began working away from home. I cut apricots and peaches for drying, and, as I got older, I sorted and hulled walnuts, hauled manure out of chicken houses, cleaned houses, worked as a secretary and a waitress, and occasionally baby-sat. None of the jobs paid very well, but what I earned helped me buy a few school clothes, occasionally go to summer church camp, and pay for other incidental expenses.

Though we never lacked food or shelter, and our few clothes were always clean and neat when we headed off for church or school, I grew up with a pervading sense of financial gloom. We only went to the doctor when absolutely necessary. The plates and flatware we used were chipped and mismatched; glasses were often old peanut butter or jelly jars. Things that other children took for granted—annual birthday parties, daily swimming in the summer, weekly trips to the movies, annual family vacations, shiny new bicycles—simply weren't possible.

As I grew older, the discrepancy between my family's income and that of other families became clearer. I felt ashamed to bring friends home, because our furniture was old and shabby. In adolescence, when clothes, hair, make-up, and boys became the primary focus of other girls' attention, I felt set apart because I could not afford the trendy "mod" mini-skirts and go-go boots or pastel angora sweaters with coordinating wool skirts that were "in" one season and "out" the next.

Yet, when I was about to enter college, not having much money paid off, at least in one sense. My family's financial situation, combined with my academic and extracurricular records, helped me receive significant scholarship assistance, enough to attend the private, church-related college I had dreamed of attending. That was a tremendous gift, and I was deeply grateful and excited about going away to school. Despite financial assistance, however, not all bills were paid, and I worked hard and lived frugally throughout my college years. At times I resented having to work while other students studied or relaxed. I often felt like a spoil sport when my roommates wanted to go out for ice cream or pizza, and I didn't have the money to go with them. I put a damper on their fun, but I felt a damper put on me as well. I was embarrassed by my lack of money, by the frugality that was necessary for me to buy books and other school supplies. I envied their money and the freedom to have fun with it.

After college, money tensions eased for a while. I landed my first job as a college admissions counselor, rented an apartment with one of my college roommates, and, with a down payment provided by a loan against my father's small life insurance policy, bought a car that would be necessary for the extensive traveling my job entailed. Though my position was by no means a lucrative one, it allowed me a financial freedom I had never experienced before.

But the challenges of money were not behind me. In the years that followed there were times of plenty and of want; times of work and of unemployment; times of relative certainty and of great anxiety. But whatever the circumstances, I always felt, in one way or another, uncomfortable about money.

As I look back on the role money played in my early years, I can identify some of the reasons I still struggle with it. The feelings and perceptions, the understandings and misunderstandings of childhood have wedged deeply into my psyche and spirit. As a youngster, I felt that I was a financial burden to my parents—so much so that when my sixth-grade class prepared to leave for its week-long science camp in the Santa Cruz Mountains, I pretended to be ill, so my parents would not have to scrape together the money for me to go. I didn't want to increase the strain on an already delicate financial situation.

As a teenager, I had no driving desire for a closet packed with clothes, but I did want more and better clothes than I had. I remember keenly my embarrassment of not having appropriate clothes for certain occasions, of wearing the same clothes over and over, of having only two sweaters—black for winter and white for summer. Yet wanting or desiring something more or something better met with mixed messages at home. My mother seemed to understand these longings; I am sure she had them herself. Often she went without decent clothing for herself in order for us kids to have school clothes or something else that we wanted or needed. The result was a feeling of gratitude permeated with guilt: why should I have a new dress when Mom doesn't have anything decent to wear?

On the other hand, my father, who had little interest in material things or for taking care of possessions, espoused the "think-of-the-starving-children-in-China" syndrome. Don't ask for anything; if you do, you're selfish. Don't complain; if you do, you're ungrateful. You are much more fortunate than many other children. And it was true, in the larger scheme of things, I was fortunate: I had shelter, food, clothing, health care, and education. But as a child, I couldn't see that larger scheme, and his response was not helpful. I didn't feel more thankful, grateful, or blessed, but only more guilty, selfish, and greedy. I also felt that my desires, my longings—whether that be for a nicer material environment or for a vocation, a wish for the future—were wrong. As I have grown older, I have often wondered if some of my father's vehemence about money came from the pressures and expectations he may have felt to be the successful breadwinner of the American Dream and his frustration at not being able to achieve that.

Throughout my childhood and youth, I learned much about money, most of it through innuendo, potent silence, and the guarded actions and conversations of my parents and other adults. But what I learned puzzled me: I was supposed to feel guilty or ashamed if I *didn't* have money; I was supposed to feel guilty and selfish if I *wanted* to have money; and, most certainly, I should feel guilty if I *did* have money! But if I did have money, in order to be a bit less selfish, I should only spend it on "practical" things or on those "less fortunate" than me. Though much of what I learned was baffling, the chief rule about money was clear: "Don't talk about it." Money, it seemed, was a secret, and a dirty one at that. Money was something scarce, difficult, painful, and embarrassing. And though the reasons for these feelings were never stated, it seemed to be because, on the one hand, there was never enough money and, on the other, money somehow was inherently evil.

Sunday school and church reinforced the sense that money was shameful at best and evil at worst: "the love of money is the root of all evils" (1 Tim. 6:10*a*, RSV), "it is easier for a camel to go through the eye of a needle than for a rich person to enter the kingdom of God" (Matt. 19:24, RSV), "sell what you have, and give to the poor" (Mark 10:21, RSV), "take heed, and beware of all covetousness; for a man's life does not consist in the abundance of his possessions" (Luke 12:15, RSV). The irony, of course, was that money was somehow acceptable if we gave it to the church for the "building up of the kingdom." Christian ethicist James B. Nelson once commented that we are taught "sex is dirty; save it for marriage." It seems we are also taught "money is dirty; give it to God."

The warnings and negativity about money and possessions seemed straightforward, definite, and indisputable. But other parts of the gospel give a different sense of money: Jesus willingly accepts financial assistance from women (Luke 8:2-3) for the support of his ministry—surely money cannot be all bad if Jesus accepts it; he joins in celebrations like the wedding at Cana, where wine flows in abundance and where, we will remember,

Jesus provides the best wine yet (John 2:1-10); he graciously receives the gift of anointing with costly oil and rebukes those who criticize the woman who anoints him (Mark 14:3-9). Even the parable of the talents in Matthew 25:14-30, while probably primarily an allegory concerning preparation for the second coming of Christ, became a story about the use and misuse of talents or money. Why was the focus at church always on the one fearful man (with whom I identified with so strongly), who buried his coin, rather than on those who used the money well? Stories of money and gifts used generously, freely, wisely, and productively are also a part of scripture, so why was the positive power of money never mentioned?

Part of the reason may be that it is always easier to avoid something complex and ambiguous than it is to muddle through it to deeper clarity and understanding. It is easier to advocate a negative attitude to wealth and possessions than to examine and acknowledge both the dangers and opportunities they offer us. The stories and sayings about money that were emphasized in my early life were the negative ones, the ones that focused on the human propensity toward evil. Those that I have just cited focus more on the human potentiality for good. We need to understand both for a realistic view of our humanity and for a realistic and healthy relationship with money.

All these stories and sayings, positive and negative, have to do with "heart": where we place our trust, what activates and animates our doing, our being, and our response to the world within and around us. Two other New Testament stories, those of the rich young man and of Zacchaeus, have helped me as I look at my own heart, especially in relation to money. A key to understanding these stories is what John Haughey refers to as "diffusion of identity," or when "what I have" and "who I am" are confused. The confusion of these two results in bondage.[1]

The rich young man (Luke 18:18-30) has outwardly observed all the commandments of God since his youth, but he confuses what he has with who he is. Jesus discerns the confusion that lies beneath his outward expression of faith, a confusion most clearly manifest in the young man's relationship with his money and possessions. Jesus asks him to give all his riches up, so he can discover who he truly is, or, we might say, so he can discover his true heart and his true relationship with God. Jesus has touched the core of the young man's existence, but he is not able to accept the invitation to freedom that Jesus offers. Instead, very sad, he turns away from Jesus. How can he give up his riches when that would mean to give up his very self? The parallel passage in Mark gives us a glimpse of Jesus' attitude toward this confused young man. Mark writes that Jesus "loved him" (10:21), a gentle reminder to us, perhaps, that Jesus calls us, lovingly and compassionately, out of our confusion to a new clarity about ourselves and our lives.

Zacchaeus (Luke 19), however, does not confuse who he is with what he has. He bilks people and he knows it. Therefore he has a freedom the young man does not have. Jesus does not ask him to give up all that he has. Instead he says, "I must stay at your house today." Jesus recognizes Zacchaeus's readiness for a change of heart. Zacchaeus scampers down from the sycamore tree and welcomes Jesus into his home, which undoubtedly is a showcase of all he has taken from others. Zacchaeus volunteers to give half of his possessions to the poor and to pay back anyone he has defrauded four times as much. Jesus responds, "Today salvation has come to this house, because he too is a son of Abraham. For the Son of Man came to seek out and to save the lost" (Luke 19:9-10). Zacchaeus is no longer lost. He has found his true heart.

Am I the young man or am I Zacchaeus? Or am I, perhaps, a little of both? Where is my heart, my true self? Do I live a life of confused grasping or clear graciousness?

Professor James Knight, a psychiatrist at Tulane School of Medicine, once said that "patients show far less resistance in relating hatred for their parents or in disclosing sexual perversities than in discussing their money status or transactions. It is as if they equated money with their inmost being."[2] If this is true, and I suspect that it often is, a serious look at our relationship with money may be a fruitful ground for spiritual self-knowledge. Perhaps money, or more precisely an examination of our relationship with it, can be a spiritual discipline, a guide for learning to live the way of faith more fully.

When I suggest that money may be a spiritual discipline, I do not mean money in and of itself. I mean money and all that is connected with it: emotions; ways of acquiring and spending money; attitudes toward it; desires for autonomy, power, independence, and status that can come with money. What, for example, do my feelings of fear, insecurity, and envy reveal about me spiritually? What do my attitudes and feelings reveal about my relationships with myself, God, and others? What are the temptations of money that need to be revealed and rejected, and the invitations that need to be recognized and accepted?

☙

Consider the lilies of the field, how they grow; they neither toil nor spin, yet I tell you, even Solomon in all his glory was not clothed like one of these. But if God so clothes the grass of the field, which is alive today and tomorrow is thrown into the oven, will he not much more clothe you—you of little faith? Therefore do not worry. . . .

Matthew 6:28*b*-31*a*

This beautiful but disturbing passage provides a starting place for delving into my own relationship with money, especially the deep fears I have about money. These verses have vexed me for years, because I seem so often to live in fear instead of in faith. Yet they console and encourage me as well, gently nudging me ever deeper into faithfulness and reminding me of God's steadfastness even in the midst of my fearfulness. Slowly I am learning that living in faith does not necessarily mean that I no longer have any fears, but that I make every effort to act faithfully, hopefully, and lovingly in the midst of and in spite of my fears.

What do I fear most about money? Very simply—not having any. But what lies beneath that? What is the fear beneath that fear? I fear being unable to care and provide for myself and those I love. And what is the fear beneath that? I fear having to ask for help. And what are the layers of fear beneath these fears? I fear being a burden. I fear being abandoned and rejected as so many people on the streets around me have been. I fear, at heart, that I will be unwanted and unloved.

But, as strange as it may seem, I am afraid not only of *not* having money; I am also afraid of *having* money. As a child I was told "money is dirty—don't put it in your mouth"; "wash your hands after touching money—you never know who might have handled it"; "money can make you sick." Can money make me sick, at least metaphorically or spiritually? Can money lure me away from what is most important in life? Slowly, insidiously would I start buying clothes I didn't really need or even want? Would I buy an expensive car or home simply for status? Would I become oblivious to my own deepest needs and the needs of the world around me?

Perhaps the fear of having money acts just as insidiously as the fear of not having money. If I believe, however unconsciously, that money is evil, that money is dirty, might that prevent me from developing gifts that God has given me, if the outcome of using those gifts might mean financial remuneration beyond what I feel is acceptable? What if, out of fear, I refuse to develop the gifts God has given me and in doing so, I negate not only my talents but also the possibility of doing much good with the money I might earn? Luke records Jesus as saying, "From everyone to whom much has been given, much will be required; and from the one to whom much has been entrusted, even more will be demanded" (Luke 12:48b). Can avoiding money, then, sometimes be a way of avoiding responsibility or of resisting God's call? Can avoiding money be a form of avoiding God?

What I often forget is that I will always need to guard against that which lures me away from the Spirit-centered life, regardless of what the external circumstances of my life may be. Likewise I must always seek to open myself to new and unexpected movements of the Spirit in whatever situation I may find myself.

Here we face the paradox of invitation and temptation. As with most things in life, money can be an invitation to fuller expressions of faithfulness, a drawing ever more deeply into the life of the Spirit, or a temptation to forgetfulness, a luring away from the life of the Spirit. This is true regardless of one's financial status or chosen way of life. Choosing to live on the edge financially in order to do essential work with those whom society has forgotten can certainly be a call to faithfulness; but it can also be motivated by or result in self-righteousness, self-absorption, and spiritual malaise. Choosing to develop interests and gifts that result in comfortable or even substantial income can do the same. Those who have inherited wealth face these same tensions. Whatever our situation, we receive invitations and face temptations. Our challenge always is to unveil self-deception and to live in the spirit of truth, to move from fear and bondage to faith and freedom.

C3

How do we move from fear to faith regarding money? How do we separate who we are from what we have? How do we move toward wisdom, freedom, generosity, and even delight and peace in dealing with money?

A starting point for me is to stop asking how *we* can do these things and to begin asking how *I* can, which is always harder than articulating what others should be doing. Perhaps that is because examining my own relationship with money reveals more of me than I care to have revealed: my fears and vulnerabilities, my greed and self-righteousness, my unspoken dreams and painful wounds. But perhaps even more deeply it reveals the fragile state of my own faithfulness and the disturbing strength of my faithlessness. Serious reflection reminds me that I have much more in common with the rich young man, who turns sadly away from Jesus, than I care to admit. Zacchaeus and I are also cronies—and not only after his change of heart, though that change is a sign of hope for me.

In the movement from fear to faith, the most difficult step for me is truly knowing and believing that who I am is not intrinsically tied to what I have or what I do. Behind that lies an even more basic step: to accept that, at the heart of existence, I am loved not for what I am but *because* I am.

Not long ago, I faced the dilemma of the rich young man in a very concrete way. I was doing freelance editing and writing from my home. My husband's salary provided our primary income, which was fine with him but which bothered me. In my adult years, before our marriage, I had always supported myself. But now I regularly battled feelings that I was not earning my keep, that I was a burden, and that I should be making much more income than I was based on my age, work experience, and education. At the same time, I was facing the need to complete a major writing project, one for which there was no guarantee of income but which I strongly felt called to do.

As I related my predicament to a friend, she asked, "What do you *need* in order to do what you want to do?" Though I hated to admit it, I replied, "I guess I would need to feel I was of worth even if I didn't bring in any income." She acknowledged my feelings with a nod, because she knew that editing was my primary source of income. But then she pushed deeper: "How much time do you need to finish the book? Can you and your husband manage on his income? How many editing and other work commitments do you already have and how long will it take you to complete them?" I answered dutifully, while sensing this might be leading me somewhere I wasn't sure I wanted to go. Then she asked another, more pointed, question: "Why don't you tell your clients you're taking a six-month sabbatical?" I laughed, a bit uneasily. "You're really pushing my edges," I said. But inside I felt both excited and scared, a combination of feelings that I have come to recognize as frequently accompanying invitations to faithfulness.

I took the sabbatical. My income dwindled to nearly nothing, and I had to face squarely how I link my income with my worth. My feelings about not earning my keep and being a burden didn't immediately vanish, but oddly, after a few months of writing, they became much less intense. I began to realize how much emotional and creative energy was wasted by my confusion of who I was with what I earned. When I realized I did not need to make excuses for not earning money, I felt not only relief but also a great release of energy to do what I felt I was called to do. I still am not totally free of the rich young man's confusion—it is very difficult to be free of it in a society such as ours—but I am freer than I used to be and that gives me hope. Jesus' love for the rich young man (Mark 10:21) heartens and reminds me that even when I confuse who I am with what I have, I am loved. I am invited to stay with Jesus that I might grow beyond my confusion, rather than turning away in sadness like the rich young man.

While the story of the rich young man compels me to look deeply within, the story of Zacchaeus challenges me to examine my relationship with the world around me. If I am loved *because* I am, others are also loved because they are. Like Zacchaeus, only when I turn in faithfulness can I experience a change of heart. That change centers my life in love, which includes looking honestly at how my life affects the lives of others.

Probably the most challenging way for this to occur regarding money is recognizing my own wealth in relation to the world as a whole. I am wealthy because I have access to adequate food, shelter, clothing, work, education, transportation, and health care. Yet it is not always easy for me to recognize that or to say that freely, usually because I compare my situation to those who have more than I do or because of my fears of what *could* happen.

But underlying my envy and my fears is something more subtle and revealing. Probably rooted in variety of experiences, ranging from my feelings as a child of not being able to do anything right to family tensions around money and to times as an adult when I barely had enough money to buy food, I have often taken refuge under the "poor me" banner. At least unconsciously I wanted people to feel sorry for me. But beneath that was a deep desire to be fully known, accepted, and loved.

It seems to me today that we often literally want to be known as "poor." We can't acknowledge our own affluence, and there is something de rigueur in our complaining about money. We can't admit that we have enough, even when deep down we know we do. Is our "poor-me-ism" a desperate plea to be known, accepted, and loved for our true selves? Is the American drive toward excessive consumption an effort to fill a very empty part of ourselves, another clue that we, like the rich young man, confuse who we are with what we have? The honest recognition of our own wealth may help us differentiate between our self-identity and our consumer-identity. And when we come to know and love ourselves for who we are, we also may be able to more fully love God and others for who they are, because they are.

We usually think of money as a personal issue, but it is not. By its very nature, money is corporate or communal. Money is worthless if it is not part of a system of exchange of materials and services among people. Wealth, monetary or otherwise, is never accomplished or accumulated solely on one's own. Therefore, how I acquire and spend my money, my wealth, always affects others. If I take living a life of faith seriously, I must carefully and honestly examine my relationship with money. Does my use of money result in good for others? When I define my own needs, am I also defining the needs of others? What happens if I say I *need* something, but then deny someone else access to the fulfillment of that same need? How we acquire and use our money has practical and spiritual ramifications. Where we do our shopping, our banking, our playing affects not only us but others as well. Our dollars are handprints of our faith, footprints of our souls.

If I carefully and honestly examine my relationship with money, I find I must also confront my fears concerning it. To know or at least to have an inkling that I am loved for who I am, helps me as I struggle to recognize and face my fears about money. This is important, because the power of fear affects not only me but others as well. When I am trapped by my fears, I may ignore larger economic and other societal problems. Fears concerning money can only exacerbate such problems, for we are never alone in our fear. As friends, as families, as communities, as nations, we face not only our own fear but the fear of others as well. We face the fear that leads to acts of discrimination and violence against groups labeled the "cause" of economic or other social problems. We face not only the fear of possible financial loss in our own lives, but the fear of desperation in the lives of those who have lost their livelihoods and, worse, their hope. Fear is not easily set aside. We deceive ourselves and sometimes mislead or abuse others when we claim that fear should be dismissed or demand that it be repressed, ignored, or denied. Fear is a symptom of a deep spiritual or psychological dis-ease; it is also a symptom of social dis-ease and disparity. We ignore it at our risk and the risk of the world around us.

But what do we do with fear, which often seems so overwhelming and all-encompassing? We face our fear and learn to live *in spite of* it, not ignoring it but rather seeking to live in faith, hope, and love in the midst of our fear. The Quaker understanding of the Light or the presence of God within has helped me as I try to act faithfully in the face of my fears. When I fear a particular situation, question, or decision, I pray silently, "Turn to the Light." This simple prayer has helped me numerous times, because it shifts the focus from my fear to the Light of faith. This doesn't necessarily mean my fears vanish, but my perspective on them changes. I see my choice clearly: I can allow the fear to permeate my actions and decisions or I can move into the graciousness of the Light. I may still feel fearful, but I can act in spite of my fear.

I once read about a woman who, with great fear, faced a difficult but necessary task. A friend urged her not to neglect the task because of her fear. Instead, she said, "Do it scared." There are times when we simply have to "do it scared." As we turn to the Light, we turn to the heart of our faith, which is love. Our turning may be clumsy, half-hearted, even confused or desperate at times, but each step toward deeper loving weakens our fears. In love we no longer confuse who we are with what we have or do not have. Likewise we no longer confuse who others are with what they have or do not have. Love opens our eyes and opens our hearts, as it did for Zacchaeus. As love increases, fear decreases, and we discover the abundance of living in grace and gratitude.

Through diligence, openness, and grace, we can move from fear to faith in dealing with money. By distinguishing between who we are and what we have, and by recognizing our material wealth, we move into the freedom that love brings. In knowing that we and all are loved, we hold a spiritual and practical wealth no one can remove. And in our daily lives, we come to know more fully the joy of satisfaction and the freedom of enough. As our love and gratitude grow, our fears subside. Our money no longer possesses us. Instead it becomes a means of expressing our faithfulness, of growing ever more deeply into the fullness that is God. ᑫ

SIX

ఆ

Trusting Nimbly: Leaning, Letting Go, and Leaping

A few years ago my husband, Greg, and I were camping in Yosemite National Park. Each day we hiked different trails, exploring the wilderness we love so much. One day, we decided to hike to the summit of 10,850-foot Mt. Hoffman.

The trail started out easily, meandering through a ragged forest of tenacious conifers that over the centuries had ground great granite slabs to coarse, gritty sand. By noon we had nearly reached the tree line, the altitude where trees no longer grow. We stopped to rest on a boulder by an alpine lake. Cupped in a great stone bowl, the still lake reflected the deep blue of the summer sky, laced here and there with wispy white clouds. Every few minutes loud, thunder-like cracks echoed off the granite walls as boulders broke free and careened down the rocky shelves. Grateful not to be in the pathway of the falling rocks, we munched on bagels, apples, and trail mix while savoring the beauty and soaking our hot feet in the icy lake.

After lunch we dried our feet, red and tingling from the lake, pulled on our heavy boots, and continued the trek upward. The trail steadily became narrower and steeper. Our pace slowed as our sea-level lungs clamored for more oxygen. Well above the tree line, we looked out across Yosemite Valley to the jagged, dark-gray peaks on its southern perimeter several miles away. We stood quietly, drinking in the pure and holy silence.

As we neared the summit, the trail leveled off and wound across an incline strewn with rocks, small boulders, and glacial debris. Marmots peeked at us from behind the rocks and scurried here and there hunting for food. We zigzagged up the slope toward a glistening snowfield, which we crunched across, pausing once or twice to throw snowballs at each other.

Nearly to the summit, we had only to scramble up a rockfall of truck-sized boulders to reach the top. A steep drop loomed below. Only then did my fear of heights kick in: my stomach tightened, my legs wavered. I felt angry, frustrated that my fear might keep me from the summit. I'd hiked this far; I wanted to go to the top, yet my fear nearly immobilized me. With much coaxing and coaching from Greg and another hiker we'd met on the way, I forced myself up and over the rocks to the summit, a large smooth mass of gently sloping rock. While Greg strolled around and peered over the precipitous edges, I sat as close to the center as I could, uneasily looking *down* on 8,852-foot Half Dome and ducking as wild-flying kites dove overhead, soaring and dipping hundreds of feet into the valley below. Their easy antics took my breath away. How I envied them.

After a brief stay, we began our descent. Greg went first. My heavy hiking boots now hindered instead of helped me. I no longer needed protection from unexpected rocks or roots on the trail; I needed flexibility. I needed to be nimble as a cat. Instead I felt like a bumbling bear as I lumbered over and edged around the huge granite boulders, trying not to think of the steep drop below me.

At one point in the descent, I halted abruptly, suspended spread-eagle on a rock. Hot panic shot through me. I could not move; I would fall if I let go. Greg assured me a good foothold was just inches away, but I could not see it. A sharp edge of granite ripped my shirt and cut into my chest. I tried to calm myself by breathing more deeply, but my panic grew.

Greg tried to encourage me. "Just move your right foot three inches more to the right and down a bit. There's a good foothold there. Let me guide your foot for you."

To move, I feared, meant to fall. But my legs were shaking and my sweaty hands were losing their grip. I couldn't see that minuscule ledge, yet I had to trust it was there.

I did make it over those rocks and down that mountain, but for several frightening moments, I didn't know that I would. I wasn't thinking about trust while I clung to that boulder. I was thinking about life—and the real possibility of death. Yet I had to trust myself, Greg, and that little ledge.

Later I realized how amazing it was for me even to be in that predicament. I don't think of myself as a big risk-taker, especially when it comes to taking physical risks. Yet the challenge to risk faces me daily. Many of those challenges, like my ascent and descent of Mt. Hoffman, center on the issue of trust: trusting myself, trusting others, trusting God.

I have always thought trusting should be easy, but it never has been for me. Yet trust comes—sometimes as gently as a cloud resting on a mountaintop and other times only after, or in the midst of, great lonely wrestling and doubt. In that resting and wrestling, God offers us the gift of a trust that is dynamic and alive, a trust that embraces leaning, letting go, and leaping.

߷

I'm not a good leaner. I strive to avoid being a burden to others, a childhood lesson I learned so well that it crippled my capacity for seeking help when I need it and for trusting others' willingness, desire, and ability to be of help. But my insistence on self-reliance has been a catch-22, because to be self-reliant I must trust myself. In learning to trust, that has been my greatest challenge: to lean on and be confident of my own understanding of people, life, and God. As a child I was not allowed or encouraged to share my questions, feelings, opinions, or fears. I learned by example that life is a private affair, to be encountered and endured alone.

Because I was expected to keep all things to myself, I assumed my thoughts and feelings were unreliable and untrustworthy. And if I could not trust myself, how could I trust others?

As I grew older, my family's privatistic approach to life blended with the North American ethic of self-reliance and rugged individualism. Somehow I was always expected to engage life on my own. Even in church, where there was talk of community and reliance on God, that individualistic strain often surfaced in an excessive emphasis on our private relationship with God. Indirectly this ethic reinforced my sense that I had to do everything alone, not only to "better" myself or to avoid burdening others, but also because others weren't to be trusted. I felt, and often still feel, overwhelmed by the expectations of "doing it all" alone, paralyzed in the face of complex personal or world challenges. On one level I deeply believe "I can do all things through [God] who strengthens me" (Phil. 4:13), yet on another I know that is not true: there are some things that can only be done, or are better done, together. And trust, I suspect, is more of a communal affair than we often realize.

I was in my twenties before I recognized that my reticence to share with people, the difficulty I had expressing my feelings and fears to others, was a sign of mistrust. That mistrust reflected not only my attitude toward others and my lack of self-trust but, perhaps more insidiously, was rooted in a mistrust of God and of life itself. The healing of that basic mistrust has occurred very slowly, and the process still continues. But the way the healing occurs is clear: it comes through facing and encountering those I fail to trust: myself, others, and God. In short, the healing comes through wrestling with life. Slowly God has led me, and continues to lead me, with great care and compassion out of the isolation of a life endured alone, alienated even from myself, toward an understanding and experience of life as a venture of trust to be celebrated and lived in communion with all of creation.

ೞ

The healing of my mistrust began with creation itself. As a child growing up in the country, my closest friends were rabbits, chickens, horned toads, lizards, fuzzy caterpillars, pollywogs, and especially cats and dogs. Filled with wonder, they opened me to life. I talked with them, sharing my hurts and my dreams, my hopes, my schemes—and they listened. I cried and they comforted me, licking the tears from my cheeks, rubbing their soft, furry bodies against mine, curling up and purring in my lap, or sitting steadfastly by my side. Even if they didn't understand or couldn't change my circumstances, they were always there.

The fertile fields and orchards also were my friends. They offered sacred space, safety, refuge. I sat for hours, under the drooping limbs of a green willow tree, watching the water course through the irrigation ditch and over the base of a concrete bridge, creating a little waterfall that filled a deep, silent pool. My soul was stilled, my spirit refreshed. I dug in the rich earth, creating palaces and forts, retreats and houses. I climbed the rough-barked almond trees, which offered me solace and refuge. Creation was dependable and good.

Creation became a bridge to people. If I could sense or see a person's love for animals or the earth, I felt, at least on some level, she or he could be trusted. Over the years, as I made human friends, I began to trust in new ways, although for many years I guarded my deepest thoughts and feelings. The first break through that barrier came when I was sixteen and fell in love for the first time. A bright, sensitive, deeply spiritual seventeen-year-old was the first person with whom I felt I could safely share my deepest self—my fears, my joys, my dreams. He held me as I cried in pain over my parents' constant bickering. He listened and did not judge me faithless when I first experienced the void, a sense of the absence of God. He shared himself with me as well. We learned together that we could trust each other with things of ultimate importance in our lives.

Through the years, friends brought more healing: my college pastor listened and supported me as I wrestled with difficult family problems and depression; college friends, by example, taught me how to hug and celebrate life; a therapist gently helped me develop a healthier sense of myself. Through these relationships, my capacity for trust continued to grow slowly and carefully.

But then I experienced a devastating breach of trust that precipitated the end of my first marriage. My fledgling ability to trust was nearly destroyed. Ironically, though, it grew stronger as I struggled through the pain and discovered that friends did not abandon me when I could not make it on my own. As I began to trust them with my anguish, I found I could more fully trust myself, because I no longer denied my deepest self. I discovered that my secret thoughts and feelings were human, understandable, acceptable. And as I leaned on my friends in openness and vulnerability, they also found it easier to lean on me; my healing was linked with theirs.

A few years later healing deepened and trust grew stronger as my friendship with Greg evolved into a committed covenant of life together. His steadfastness in difficult times, his willingness to wrestle through confusion and pain while remaining confident of God's presence, and his deep love for me nurtured trust. Marriage is a profound act of trust. And trust, nourished by love, continues to grow. That growing trust allowed me to lean on him when my life depended on him.

Over the years I have learned there is a mutuality or reciprocity to trust. Like Greg, my other human and creature friends created an environment in which trust could grow. As they offered themselves to me, they also offered me an experience of the trustworthy God. Like my creature and human friends, God stands by me, listening and loving without reservation. Like the trees and fields, God offers rich gifts of solace and refuge, of sacred places that heal and refresh.

Trust does not exist in a vacuum. It is relational. It binds and intertwines us with the human and the Holy, to creation and all the created, and to all our experiences with them. Those who guide us up, over, and around the boulders and chasms of our lives reveal the many faces of God. Sometimes God seems to be no more than a ledge, a tenuous foothold when we struggle to keep our balance as the world weighs heavily upon us. We may panic when we can't see that ledge, but it is there. Somehow we will be guided to it. We are held in the heart and hands of God when we least feel it. The ledge of God will hold us, and, perhaps because of its seeming tenuousness, it encourages us to take the necessary next step.

⋈

That day on Mt. Hoffman, my capacity to lean on and to trust Greg was built on prior leanings in which he had proved trustworthy. But I could not lean forever. Even though my grip on the rock became more precarious when he grasped my boot, loosening it from a narrow crevice, I had to let go. Greg's trust in me, his confidence that I could and would release my grasp even in the face of great fear, helped me trust myself. Those three inches seemed like three long yards as I fought to keep my balance and composure while Greg inched my boot across the rough rock to the new foothold. Then I had to let go. I could not leap to a new place or continue my journey if I did not let go.

As we lean and let go, our self-trust intertwines with our trust of others and of God and opens us up to life. But what allows us to let go and open up to life, especially in the face of doubt and fear? More than we realize, our images of God affect our ability or inability to trust. They help us lean, let go, and leap—or they hold us back. The images of God I learned as a child were mixed. God was wrathful and judgmental, but also gentle and loving—a schizophrenic tension guaranteed to make trusting difficult and problematic. I feared God, yet in some uncanny way I sensed I was safe praying to, talking to, and being with God. God was present—though I doubt I could have articulated this as a child—in creation, which was trustworthy.

Thus I made an unspoken, intuitive connection between the trustworthiness of creation and of God. As I grew older, I discarded my image of God as a wrathful, judgmental old man "up there." When I embraced new images—God as Creator, Source, Ground of Being, Matrix of All Life—and reclaimed the old image of a gentle, loving God, trusting God became easier. I found comfort in the knowledge that God was beyond all images. No human image could encompass or fully express the immensity and totality of God. And yet, life also revealed glimpses of the personal God—the listener, the steadfast friend, the healer. This was a God who could be trusted. This God would support me when I leaped.

I cringe when people talk about trusting God in tones of total abdication and abnegation, as if trusting God were a way to escape the complexities of life. Somehow in their eyes we are little remote-controlled cars that God guides along a freeway bypassing the busy, frustrating, clogged intersections of life. It's easy to judge these people, perhaps because I am so often like them. I sometimes want God to be the benevolent dictator or overprotective parent. I trust God to take care of everything so I don't have to do anything. I resist using my intellect, my intuition, my heart. I trust God so I can keep my distance from life, from grappling with the uncertainties, complexities, and grunginess of living in faith each moment of the day. I trust God to take care of everything so I can vegetate—or more piously, meditate. At times I am lazy and I want God to happen "to" me rather than encountering and engaging God in life. When I say I want to trust God, do I really mean I want God to protect me from the bumps, bruises, and challenges of life? But doesn't trusting God mean trusting that God is present even in the hard times, even when we don't "feel" trustful?

What about those times when we simply cannot trust—those times when we are so overcome with pain, brokenness, alienation, or betrayal that we lose our courage and strength to trust? For me this most clearly happened during my divorce. It was then that I had to lean on the community of faith that surrounded me. My community of faith was, and often still is, a community in dispersion. My local congregation, for whatever reasons, did not or could not support me at that time. Friends and family, near and far, composed my faith community. They stood with me and for me; they were my advocates with God and God's advocates with me.

When we are unable to trust, the community trusts for us and with us. When we let go, we are held by others and by God, in faith, in prayer, in hope. The community, through its covenant with God, keeps the possibility of trust and hope alive. The community reassures us that trust *is*; its existence is not contingent on our personal ability or inability to trust at any given moment. The community holds, as the foundation of all other trust, the ultimate trustworthiness of God. In this way the community supports us as we let go and leap. Through the community of faith, God leads us out of isolation and privatism to full engagement with life. We trust God when we are able to let go, despite our pain and fears, and leap into life.

൦ଃ

To trust we lean, let go, then leap for life. Trust is, among other things, a yearning for that which is beyond. As I clung to that rock on Mt. Hoffman, I yearned for life. I longed to leap from my precarious perch to the wide, steady path of solid rock. I longed to bridge the chasm and go on living.

What is this yearning for life? It is a yearning for God and for the fullness of God's presence, of God's reign, vibrant and alive within us and the world. We anticipate the coming of God's reign by living *as if* it already existed. We lean, let go, and leap, trusting that God will be faithful and learning that God's reign is real in that very moment. This does not mean that life will be perfect or that our leaping will always be graceful and our landings easy. It means that God is present and faithful; in that moment, the reign of God is already here. But God's reign is also not yet complete. Daily we experience brokenness and incompleteness in ourselves and in the world. We live a life that is *already but not yet.*

Trusting is an anticipatory act. It bears witness to that which remains to be fully realized. Why is that kind of witness important for our common life? Trusting creates conditions favorable to the fulfillment of God's reign, to the creation of a new heaven and a new earth. As we trust, our trusting creates the conditions for more trust, for more reciprocity and mutuality. Our trust becomes the salt that flavors the world, that enhances the best in people. Our trust is the leaven that enables us to live with our neighbors in peace, to bend our swords into plowshares, to make the dry lands springs of water, to turn from death to life.

Trust is the meeting point of the *already* and the *not-yet* of God's reign. We know it in its most exhilarating and frightening form when we take the leap of faith and find ourselves suspended in midair. We are propelled toward newness but also fear falling into the chasm below. We are able to trust because God helps us move into and through our human limitations and brokenness, the experiences of broken trust in intimate relationships, the lack of nurturing in childhood, all that binds and scars us with mistrust. Our scars remind us of the ways we and our world fall short of the reign of God, but they also testify to God's healing power. It is important to acknowledge their existence, but they no longer need impede us. Scar tissue is strong, but often rigid and unyielding. God releases the fear that we have learned through pain and broken trust, the fear that rigidifies and immobilizes us. This release frees us to draw on our strengths and to move more fully into life.

We choose to trust, remembering that the source of our trust is God, the divine matrix of all that is holy, whole, and healing. But mature trust has open eyes; it is not naïve. The paradox of the *already* and the *not-yet* remains. We will still experience the breaking of trust. At times others will betray our trust; we will betray theirs, and perhaps even our own. In spite of these searing stabs of brokenness, we strive to trust, confident that God is present with us in our pain, doubts, and mistrust—

just as God (and Greg) was present with me on Mt. Hoffman. It is this that makes God trustworthy: Emmanuel—God with us. God is trustworthy because God is wholly present with us in each moment of our lives—in our pain, our doubts, our mistrust. God is with us through our Egypts and our wilderness wanderings; through our long nights of lonely wrestling and the trial of false accusations; through our crucifixions and our resurrections. Trust is not a naive act of denial or repression; it is a movement out of the past, into the present, and toward the future—toward healing, life, and hope.

Trust is not for the squeamish. Through God's grace we often leap—sometimes nimbly, sometimes not—when we least expect to leap. Sometimes we trust when we have "no choice," when we're up against the wall or out on the ledge. Yet we *choose* to trust. Our leaping, uncertain and precarious as it may sometimes feel, is an incarnation of trust. This raw-edged trust pushes us on despite our fear. We act in faith *as if* we trust, and in doing so, trust emerges. Trust is a courageous act (from the Old French, *cuer*, heart), an act of the heart.

Yet trust is paradoxical. The Chinese character for the word *crisis* includes the characters for *danger* and *opportunity*. In the crisis of trust, we face the danger of losing all trust, of losing faith, but we are also offered the opportunity to strengthen and enlarge our capacity to trust. We yearn both for the beyondness and for the at-home-ness, the refuge of God. As we leap and move into the beyond, we discover that the boundaries of that at-home-ness keep expanding. With each leap, we are invited further into the spaciousness of God's love. As Emily Dickinson once wrote, "We both believe and disbelieve a hundred times an hour which keeps Believing nimble."[1] And so it is with trust. May our trusting be nimble. ♋

III

☙

Being, Becoming, and Blessing

♋

The long night is nearly over. Jacob turns toward the east, squinting his weary eyes. Is the horizon brightening, he wonders, or am I just imagining it? He relaxes a bit. Then a voice cuts through the darkness around him: "Let me go, for the day is breaking." Jacob tightens his grip and replies, "I will not let you go, unless you bless me" (Gen. 32:26).

Can we be as bold (or perhaps as desperate) as Jacob to demand a blessing from our struggles and our God? What might that mean? For Jacob, it required a transformation of self. Blessing comes for Jacob only after he has offered his name (a symbol of who he most deeply is) to the one with whom he has struggled, the one who now names him anew. The change is deep. It is not simply a change of letters from J-a-c-o-b to I-s-r-a-e-l. Jacob changes as a person. The focus of his life shifts as he awakens to who he truly is and who he can be when he lives his life wholly in relationship with God. The blessing draws forth the divine image that lies deep within him, a power so real that Jacob can now risk reconciliation with Esau.

Jacob's experience echoes my own deep desire to discover the Holy within all of life, to be touched and named anew, to receive the blessing of God that draws forth the divine image within me.

SEVEN

On Having Faith—In Failure

A few years ago I received an invitation to my twenty-year high school reunion. In many ways, I wanted to go. I attended a small school in a rural, agricultural area of Central California about ninety miles east of San Francisco. My senior class had 118 students, and we all knew each other. It would be good to see everyone again.

But as I contemplated going, I was hounded by an honor bestowed on me by my peers as a high school senior. Along with a male classmate, I had been voted "Most Likely to Succeed." Twenty years later I most certainly did not meet the usual criteria of success. I didn't have a high-powered, high-paying job or a prestigious academic appointment; I didn't drive a fancy car or wear designer clothes. I didn't own an expensive home; in fact, I didn't own a home at all.

What, I wondered, did I have to show for the twenty years since high school? College and graduate degrees, yes, but not—at least in the eyes of many—in anything practical. I had professional experience in public relations and academic administration, but I also had some extended periods without work when I scraped to make ends meet. At the time of the reunion, I was working as a free-lance editor and writer, which—except for the generosity of my husband, who kept encouraging me in my fledgling career while paying most of the bills—did not even pay the rent. I had published a few articles and book reviews, but none in magazines my classmates were likely to know. The reunion invitation stirred up feelings of failure, inadequacy, and incompetency, feelings I had struggled with much of my life.

In addition to feelings of professional failure, I still carried the scars from the failure of my first marriage several years earlier. Though I knew many of my classmates also had experienced divorce, I still occasionally felt the sting of that failure and the stigma that goes with it. Time had healed most of the wounds, but memories of the divorce were still clear: the overwhelming sense of failing to love and to be loved; my seeming inability to be in relationship in a healthy and creative way; the guilt, disappointment, and disillusionment of breaking a commitment considered sacred.

Despite the fact that I had experienced much healing, had married again, and was beginning to make small inroads into the work I had always wanted to do, at times I still felt keenly the pain of not measuring up, of not accomplishing anything of real value in my life, of not being who I somehow was supposed to be. Failures, real and perceived, hung heavily over me. Ironically, to others I had often appeared to be a success, while inwardly I felt myself to be an utter failure.

At some point in our lives, I think most of us wrestle with failure or feelings of failure. The source may vary—reflections on work done or undone, a faltering business or unsuccessful job interview, family difficulties, academic deficiencies, spiritual malaise. Whatever the source, failure and the feelings of failure touch us at our very core and cause us to ask: Who am I? What can I do? What am I worth? We wrestle with the consequences of our failures—finding new directions, straining to make ends meet, binding up what has been broken. But sometimes we struggle even more with our feelings of and about failure. For it is how we perceive and feel about our failures that activates anxiety, absorbs energy, and influences the concrete responses we make.

ℭ

For years I could not escape my feelings of failure, of being a failure. They pursued me, hung over me, haunted and taunted me: "You can't do anything right," "There is something wrong with you," "You're no good and you never will be."

Where did these strong feelings come from? Although the origins of feelings are complex, I can identify several factors that have played a part in my struggle. They involve my immediate community (including my most immediate "community," myself) and the larger community, or culture, in which I grew up, the United States.

At home, I felt nothing I did was good, or even good enough. Since pride was viewed as the ultimate sin and emotions or affection rarely expressed, encouragement and praise were nearly nonexistent. In school, competition was the main mode of encouragement and, though I fared better than many children because I was an apt and diligent student, I quickly grew to believe nothing less than an "A" was acceptable; a "B" was a sign of failure. And in church each Sunday I was reminded over and over that I was "sinful and unclean." Although grace was revered dogmatically, in practice it paled, seemingly ineffectual and impotent, in the face of sin.

I also held exorbitantly high expectations of myself. I see now that my perfectionism, which thankfully has eased a bit through the years, was an effort to be in control when I felt powerless and out of control. Through my actions (grades, school accomplishments, work), I was attempting to gain the love and acceptance of my family, friends and acquaintances, and perhaps even God, who, it often seemed, was convinced of my total depravity. I feared letting my true imperfect self be known, for surely then I would be rejected. There was no way, I believed, that people or even God could love me unless I was perfect.

My experiences at home, school, and church wove into the larger fabric of North American culture. The top side of this fabric revealed a colorful mix of initiative, "can-do" spirit, and derring-do. This land of opportunity often rewarded individual initiative and hard work handsomely, at times even despite one's economic, ethnic, educational, or racial background. If I just worked hard enough, the American myth said, I would succeed, financially and otherwise. But there was and is an underside to American culture as well, a side that has often reinforced my feelings of failure. Here image is tantamount, success—particularly material success—is revered, and failure is ignored, denied, and denigrated. Mistakes are not allowed and must be quickly and literally erased from our lives; all must be perfect, upbeat, positive. Our primary goal is to reach "the top of the heap," to be "bigger and better" than everyone else. It doesn't really matter how we succeed as long as we do succeed in some visible, preferably spectacular, way. This land of opportunity is also the land of opportunism.

The popular culture that surrounded me while I grew up, particularly radio, TV, and movies, promoted these themes through programming, story lines, characterization, and advertising. Tapping directly into the image of America as the land of opportunity, the advertising industry advanced the cause of the American Dream. The advertising of the 1950s and 60s (when I was growing up) pales in comparison with the intensity, sophistication, and magnitude of today's advertising. Yet it set the tone for the "good life," a life that now, if we are to believe advertisers, is achieved less by initiative and hard work than by acquisition or consumption of particular products.

Those of us who live in this land of plenty are bombarded daily with hundreds, even thousands, of alluring images promising everything from popularity to serenity, sexual fulfillment to perfect family life, power to prestige. We can buy and own "Prestige" and "Infiniti" in the form of sleek new cars. Our underwear can—and *should,* advertising implies—be more than underwear; it can be an "under*statement.*" "Eternity" is contained in a bottle with which we scent our lives. If only we consume what we are offered, we will be an instant success.

In so many words, or more precisely, images, we are told that unless we buy these jeans, eat this cereal, and drive that car, we are inadequate, deprived, "out of it"; we are, in short, failures. We are also told, subtly and incessantly, that we can be "better"— more beautiful, more powerful, more envied, more successful—if we buy all these things. Advertising, therefore, pits us not only against ourselves but against others as well. Our insecurities help fuel consumption, because if we do not project the latest image, we may be ridiculed, discarded, or rejected like poodle skirts and the Edsel.

No longer valued for who we are, we are valued for what we use. The American variation on Descartes's theme has become "I consume, therefore I am," despite the fact that our consumption literally denies others their fair share of the world's resources, destroys the planet upon which our survival depends, and leaves us feeling spiritually empty. We are what we consume. And in order to get us to consume more and more of things we need less and less, advertisers aim at our most vulnerable spots: our need and desire to be loved and accepted, to have a sense of meaning and purpose, to have some semblance of power in a world where we often feel insignificant and powerless.

The power and ubiquity of advertising, the American emphasis on the self-made person, and the cult of success create a formidable challenge to those of us who seek to live our lives in the image of the Creator rather than the image of Madison Avenue, to those who seek to work toward creating "a new heaven and a new earth" rather than consuming the ones we already have. The pressure to conform to and take on the image of the world around us is great.

How many of our experiences and feelings of failure are rooted in cultural values that are skewed and dehumanizing, values that exalt quantity over quality, objects over personhood, products over producer? What if at least part of the reason we feel we are failures is that we are exactly where we should be? As John Francis Kavanaugh put it, "It should not come as a surprise that a follower of Jesus might find himself or herself to be an outsider in a culture dominated by the commodity. It should be no shame to feel different, even to feel a bit disjointed and out of place, in a civilization that divinizes the thing."[1] If we as people of faith believe that humans, not things, are made in the image of God, what might failure mean for us? Can failure help us move away from the hollowness of the world and more deeply into life, more fully into the way of the Spirit? Can we "have faith" in failure?

⊂઩

We shun failure and other seemingly negative experiences because we fear that revealing our weaknesses and imperfections will render us unlovable, unacceptable, and, in today's lingo, unmarketable. Failure is simply taboo, which may be one reason why we have such difficulty as a nation accepting the great failures of our society that have resulted in poverty, homelessness, illiteracy, violence, crime, and the growing gap between rich and poor. Failure exposes our vulnerability. But failure is also part of our humanity. By avoiding failure, we avoid our own humanity, and in avoiding our humanity, we avoid and deny our very selves, the most precious gift God has given us.

Our humanity challenges us to recognize that life is gift and that even difficulties may have something important to offer us. A child learns to walk by trying, failing, and trying again. A scientist postulates theories and designs experiments, which often fail. Yet in failing they may reveal more than if they had succeeded. An artist, in combining materials, colors, and personal vision, may experience repeated failures, each of which is essential to the painting that finally emerges. Failures, mistakes, or therapeutic errors, as they are sometimes called, are one of the ways we learn to live life more fully.

In view of society's attitude, failure actually may be one of the greatest spiritual disciplines or ways of learning how to live the en-Spirited life. Yet, we must be careful not to romanticize or spiritualize failure, because failure—particularly profound, prolonged, or repeated failure, or failure devoid of hope—can crush the human spirit. When we are raw and vulnerable, we may be wounded even more deeply, because all our defenses are down. Here, whether dealing with ourselves or others, we do well to proceed with great gentleness and deep care. Failure should not be brushed aside, belittled, or trivialized. Yet failure, for all its harshness and darkness, may lead us to the light. This is the time when, because of our neediness and poverty, we are often most open and receptive to the movement of the Spirit.

One of my favorite "Peanuts" cartoons shows Sally sitting at a table with two pieces of paper, one large and one small, in front of her. As she writes diligently on the large piece, she says to Charlie Brown, "I'm making a list of all the things I've learned in life. . . . Well, actually I'm making two lists." Charlie Brown asks, "Why is one list longer than the other?" Holding up the long list, Sally says, "These are the things I've learned the hard way!"

That cartoon pretty much sums up my experience, particularly my experience with failure. I've learned a lot "the hard way," not only because at times I can be hard-headed, but also because I think that's the way life often is. Perhaps we are more attentive when life is hard. When we are open and vulnerable, the Spirit can more easily lead us forth to fuller expressions of wisdom, compassion, and love—to the heart of our humanity, the *imago Dei*, the image of God. Yet how hard it is to be open, to stretch our spirits, worn and fragile from the pain of failure, so that we may receive an even greater measure of God's love and comfort. Like most other experiences, we won't learn from failure if we don't encounter it, embrace it, live *through* it open-heartedly, reflectively, intentionally, expectantly.

ᘓ

But how can we enter into failure and learn from it? For me, reflection and prayer have been essential for embracing my failures and learning from them.

Healthy reflection is a paradox. It requires both a full entering into the thoughts, feelings, and realities of failure, but also a distancing or detachment from them. We must acknowledge our failure without becoming trapped in it. Reflection helps us remain responsible, "able to respond," to the practical, emotional, and spiritual demands of failure by helping us sort through the truths and untruths we and others may tell us about our specific failure and about failure in general.

Failure offers the opportunity to look at important questions: Who am I? What are my gifts? How do I want to live my life? We wrestle with our own uniqueness, discovering how we differ from others. This is particularly bewildering when we lose confidence in our gifts, feel we don't have any or don't know what they are, or discover that our gifts aren't valued by society, church, or those close to us, including ourselves. We face the need to love ourselves, which often includes struggling with envy or jealousy toward others whose lives seem easier and more successful than our own.

Reflection is both a solitary and a communal act. Communally it may take the form of friendship, spiritual direction, pastoral counseling, therapy, social analysis and critique, or reading and responding to that reading. Sharing our experiences of failure with those who know and love us provides care and encouragement in an often barren time. It provides a "reality check," a means of discriminating between real and perceived failures, of balancing the expectations of a faithful life with the expectations of the society around us. Here reflection intersects with critique as together we examine the standards that we, societally and personally, use to determine failure or success and as we explore how we might live a life of gospel faithfulness in the world.

In the midst of reflection, prayer gathers us into a posture of yearning for truth about ourselves, others, the world, and God. Its focus is on being, becoming, blessing—not on having, possessing, consuming. In prayer we encounter God intimately and God gently reminds us, "You are precious in my eyes, and honored, and I love you" (Isaiah 43:4*a*, RSV). Prayer not only provides solace in our pain, but quiets our spirits so we may move past surface answers and self-deception to hear the heart of our deepest desire, the heart of God within us.

Prayer draws us into the sacred truth—which often runs counter to what we are told by the world—that we are loved and accepted, that our sense of meaning and purpose grows out of our sacred connection with God, life, and all that is, and that the power we have is the power of the Spirit within us, a presence and power that is gift, a presence and power that the world cannot remove.

By entering into my own failures through reflection and prayer, I've learned some basic lessons about living. One of the most helpful lessons is a surprising one: failure can be a relief. When I could honestly admit, without denigrating myself, that I could never be perfect, I could finally get off my own back. In doing so, I became freer to use and explore the gifts God gave me. I became more accepting of my work and more willing to try new things. This freedom allowed a new creativity and generativity to emerge, not only in my work itself but *within* me as well. I became less judgmental, more compassionate, more encouraging. Others' weaknesses were no longer indictments of my own weaknesses but possible places for healing, cooperation, and growth.

Another lesson I am slowly learning is that I sometimes confuse incompleteness with failure. Living in this instant-gratification, quick-fix society can easily warp our sense of appropriate timing. Not everything can or should happen *now*. I have to learn to grow into myself, into my work, into the world around me. Becoming is a part of life. When we too quickly label ourselves or others "failures" because something in our lives has not yet come to fruition, we may stunt the growth of ourselves and our gifts. We need to give ourselves and one another time to become—time, perhaps, even to be created.

Failure also challenges me to remember my own salvation history, to recognize and acknowledge the movement of the Spirit throughout my life. Failure reminds me to look back with thanksgiving for God's faithfulness in the past and forward in anticipation of a greater sense of the Holy in the future. Failure then invites me to gather both the past and the future into the present moment, that I may live fully and faithfully now.

Failure, real or perceived, taps into our fears that we are not acceptable, worthy, valuable, lovable. The challenge of failure is to remain faithful in the midst of those fears, in the mire and muck of pain, grief, loss, disappointment, embarrassment, insecurity, or uncertainty—be it financial, personal, or spiritual. To be faithful does not mean to ignore, discount, repress, or deny failure or our feelings about it. Being faithful in failure means opening ourselves up even further, so we may readily receive God's love and be salved by God's healing compassion. In response we are graced still further as we ourselves grow in wisdom, compassion, and love.

෪

As we wrestle with failure, we need to remember we are in good company. Jesus failed too. The problem with being on this side of the resurrection is that we often miss the pain and anguish of the failure that preceded it. In the eyes of the world, Jesus' life and ministry were most certainly failures. He did not change the hearts of all who heard him, nor did he usher in a visible reign of God on earth. To those who expected a sociopolitical savior, he failed to liberate Palestine from Roman rule. He even failed to gain the loyalty of his disciples, who abandoned him and denied having any association with him. He died a humiliating, lonely, and painful death, taunted and ridiculed for being who he truly was. And yet . . .

As people of faith, we need to remember that the resurrection tosses out all standard expectations and measurements of failure and success. Neither failure nor success in and of itself is good or evil; either can result in growth, stagnation, or regression. In our struggle with failure and success, we may find a hidden strength as we commend our spirits to our Creator and seek to yield our lives to love. Our challenge is to have faith—in failure, in success, in whatever life brings. The unexpected turns, the painful endings, the precarious beginnings are all part of the path of faith, where we are reminded with each step that the resurrection did not happen only once long ago, it happens each day of our lives. ⟡

EIGHT

A Questing, Questioning Faith

T he thread of faith—fragile yet resilient, delicate yet strong—is what binds all my wrestlings together. Faith weaves strength, power, and hope into my life even when I feel weak, powerless, or hopeless. But what is this faith? Why do I often struggle with faith itself?

I find it difficult to define faith. Yet over the years, I have come to hold that, perhaps at its most basic, faith is living in trust that there is something beyond my own understanding, something larger of which I am a part. This something beyond helps bring order, significance, and purpose to my life. Faith gives me hope that beyond each night, dawn awaits. Faith reminds me that each moment is sacred and that every creature, every person is intimately connected with life. All that is, is an integral, irreplaceable part of creation.

I believe this faith, this living in trust, is active and dynamic. It engages us in all that we do and in all that we are. Faith works within us, beckoning us, urging us, encouraging us to live life fully and abundantly—to live, to love, and to be loved.

But what happens when this neat understanding of faith encounters the ragged edges—the ambiguities, uncertainties, and complexities—of my daily life? What happens when living and loving and being loved confront the rawness of a crumbling relationship or a meaningless death? What happens when it seems impossible to love others, because I can't even love myself?

113

Beliefs – about what we believe about ⊕.
Faith – what ⊕ believes about us.

What does it mean, concretely and practically, for me to live, to love, and to be loved?

I have many questions, and, for me, faith and questions go hand in hand. Slowly I am discovering that living a life of faith may not mean as much to know the answers as it means to embrace the questions, or as the poet Rainer Maria Rilke put it "to live" and "to love" the questions. But what does it mean to live and to love the questions? I think, most basically, it means to live and to love life.

At its heart, the spiritual journey is a quest to live and love fully. Our questions help us grow, deepen, and ripen in our faith and in our living. They challenge and prod us, fluster and vex us. But if we live *with* and *into* our questions, we may, again as Rilke so gracefully rendered it, "gradually without noticing it, live along some distant day into the answer."[1]

My spiritual quest has generated many questions over the years. These questions, both articulated and unarticulated, have molded my experience and understanding, just as my experience and understanding have elicited new questions. At times, I feel I have begun to live into an answer or two. But I have much, much more "living into" to do. Questions have always been a part of my life, and I expect they always will be. And maybe, just maybe, the questions are as important, or even more so at times, than the answers themselves.

⚬

As a child, I learned that there were "appropriate" questions and "inappropriate" questions. Appropriate questions elicited answers that reinforced proper, or socially acceptable, behavior. Inappropriate questions, like inappropriate or incorrect answers, brought shame or ridicule, or were stonily ignored. I quickly learned not to ask many questions and to make those I did ask, appropriate ones, just as I learned to make my answers appropriate. But once, giving an appropriate, proper answer backfired.

When I was about nine years old, a man who served as a chaplain at San Quentin State Prison taught my Sunday school class for several weeks. How he ended up teaching in my little church, in a rural area more than two hours away from the prison, I still don't know. But he did. One sunny Sunday morning, my class sat in a circle on cool metal folding chairs in our usual meeting place, the church kitchen. After opening prayer, Pastor H. asked, "Is God everywhere?" Years of Sunday school and church had primed us for this. We knew the answer: "Yes," we responded without hesitation. In a flash, he thrust his hand into mid-air, grabbing here and clutching there, as he taunted, "Is God here? Is he here? Or here?" Sheepishly, we said no. "Well," he said, "if God is everywhere, why isn't he here?"

I don't recall anything else about the class, but I do remember going home that day feeling my faith had been mocked and my spirit bruised. His intentions, I suspect, were admirable—to help us grow in faith—but his approach was not. His question may have been appropriate at a later age, but he obviously knew little about nourishing and nurturing faith in children. Even at that tender age I knew he didn't understand or respect the faith that was deep within me. Instead he tried to wrench that faith out and force it into his understanding, into his categories. From him, among others, I learned to be careful what I said about my faith, not only about what I asked but also what I answered.

Yet this disturbing encounter with its riveting question—is God everywhere?—remained with me. The question pointed to a truth that took me years to grasp, an answer that it took years to live into: although we may believe that God (or whatever we name the holy power that undergirds and enlivens all that is) is everywhere, God cannot be contained in our categories, grasped in our hands, or fully understood. Perhaps, then, it is part of the nature of God to cause us humans to ask questions. If nothing else, our questions continually remind us that God is always more than any of our answers.

Questions became more important in my teens, if for no other reason than I had many more of them. I became suspicious of people, especially adults, who were unwilling to answer questions or who had pat answers for everything. Somehow, however unwittingly, I sensed that questions were meant to be honored, but that didn't necessarily mean they could or should always be answered. Questions, it seemed, touched on the very mystery of life. I began to respect people who had the courage to admit they didn't know all the answers, people who could say, "Maybe . . ." or "I don't know."

When I was about fifteen, my Sunday school class studied a book that dealt with various practical, ethical issues from a Christian perspective. The teacher was autocratic and inflexible, so we discussed very little. Questions simply provided the teacher with a forum for expounding his beliefs and opinions, his understanding of how young people should be trained in the ways of faith. Soon we stopped asking questions. Each class became an exercise in endurance as we were preached at instead of being encountered in our faith. Then came the chapter on sex. The teacher, a bit uneasily I suspect, told us we could read that chapter on our own, and as a class we would go on to the next chapter. I couldn't accept the avoidance of important issues, such as sexuality, in the context of faith. If Sunday school was not going to deal with real stuff, if we couldn't ask questions honestly and deal with them in their complexity, I decided Sunday school wasn't worth attending. So I refused to go any longer, much to the bewilderment, embarrassment, and frustration of my parents.

The end of Sunday school by no means marked the end of my faith quest, though it came to a painful, abrupt halt about two years later. The summer I was seventeen I read James Michener's *The Source*, a novel that, among other things, probes the development of monotheism from its roots in prehistoric Middle-Eastern expressions to its contemporary Judeo-Christian and Islamic manifestations. As I read about the nameless monolith, erected by prehistoric peoples to placate nature and protect their crops, evolving into other religious and cultic expressions, it seemed to me that people were creating God in their own minds. Was God simply a figment of human imagination? I wondered. If people could "create" God, I reasoned, then God didn't exist. My faith, which had been the foundation of my life, crumbled. Only a void, a pit of nothingness, remained. I shared my anguish with my boyfriend, who held me and listened as I wrestled, questioned, and cried. I couldn't talk to my pastor or any adult—I was certain I would be labeled a heretic or chastised for my lack of faith.

One hot summer night, at a loss as to what to do, my boyfriend suggested we go to his church to pray, and if I couldn't pray, just to be. We slipped into the dark, silent church and sat in a back pew. The air was close and dull, deadened by the heat. I could see nothing. Occasionally the building groaned; otherwise silence surrounded us. Nothingness weighed heavily on me. I waited and waited; for what, I didn't know. Foolish as I felt addressing a God who seemed not to exist, I still prayed, "God, if you exist, somehow let me know." I sat on the hard wooden pew, waiting in feeble hope and in dull dread. What if God answers, I wondered. Or worse, what if God doesn't answer? Finally, after a long time had passed, we stepped out of the church into the clear, warm ebony night and looked up at countless sparkling stars. Something inside me shifted the wrestling and emptiness of the past days and weeks to a new place. Gently, almost imperceptibly, the weight lifted, and in the silence I sensed the gracious presence of God.

But I could never go back to where I had been before, to the faith I had held before. At the time, I didn't realize that my questions and my doubts were stretching my faith and understanding, giving them a new spaciousness within which to grow. The silent assurance, unspoken and unspeakable, that followed the stretching graciously affirmed this new and holy space. Exposed to a story of faith that seemed so unlike my own, a story of a people seeking a connection with the source, with the Holy, in ways that seemed so very different from my own seeking, I at first could only conclude that if God didn't exist solely within my experience of faith, life, and culture, then God didn't exist at all. My doubts and confusion sent me plummeting into the void. But instead of leading me away from faith, this difficult experience deepened, broadened, and heightened both my faith and my understanding of it. Terrifying in its intensity and ultimacy, that bald question—"Does God exist?"—was unutterably answered with a silent assurance, "Yes," and an ever-challenging revelation, "In ways you cannot yet imagine or comprehend."

CB

Intertwined with my questions regarding the existence of God were questions about the doctrines and mores of my tradition. Was Jesus really resurrected from the dead? What does that mean? Why are other faiths considered wrong? Are they? What does it mean that "God is love"? I remember sitting in my bedroom one day, reading from my new Bible, *Good News for Modern Man*, with its whimsical line drawings and then-contemporary language. I came to a verse I had heard so often that the words rolled off my tongue by rote: "God is love." But this time I read the words hungrily, again and again. I looked out my window, across the apricot orchard, beyond our neighbor's pasture to the dark-blue outline of the mountains on the western rim of the valley. With simplicity and unspeakable clarity, a new understanding grasped me: these weren't just words. This wasn't just a nice, "warm-fuzzy" Bible verse to be memorized and spouted on cue. This had something to do with the very essence, the very beingness of God. God was connected directly and completely with life—*and* with loving.

At eighteen, I went away to college, a small, church-related liberal arts school in Southern California. It was a good place for me, small enough to know people but large enough to expose me to a world of culture, religion, politics, and the arts that I had not known before. My college years began at the tail end of the turbulent sixties. The Vietnam War was still raging, minority rights advocates were gaining a voice and an audience, and feminism, or "women's lib," was articulating women's experience and roles in new and often controversial ways. "Rap groups" proliferated as quickly as nuclear weapons, and "consciousness-raising" was the politically and psychologically correct thing to do.

It was a compelling, challenging, and often confusing time. Friends, especially those who could help me or simply be with me in my questioning, became essential companions on my journey of faith. One new friend was my campus pastor, who, I soon learned, was not afraid of questions, "appropriate" or "inappropriate." He quickly became a spiritual guide and mentor as I wrestled with new ways of thinking, the challenges of relationships, and the meaning of faith in the midst of so much uncertainty and newness. Here in the rich mix of the college experience, I learned that the realm of faith included all of life— the intellectual, political, social, interpersonal, cultural, and intercultural. All was intimately connected with the spiritual.

Among many other things, I learned I could question authority and that those in power are not always right (nor, in contrast to what many others believed, are they always wrong). Slowly I gained an awareness that symptoms such as drug or alcohol abuse, while quite serious problems in themselves, are not necessarily the heart of societal ills. Conversations with women faculty and students, and my reading of Betty Friedan's *The Feminine Mystique*, raised questions about the traditional role of women in the world—and by extension, my role in the world— including the world of faith. If God loved all people, why were women and minorities treated unequally in society and even in the church? If the house of God was to be a "house of prayer for all people," why were there such visible and vicious divisions between various denominations and faiths? My worldview broadened and I began to question whether the United States, whites, males, and other dominant power groups were always right and their assessments of others accurate.

After graduation, I worked as a college admissions officer for three years, and then entered a Master of Divinity program at a Protestant seminary. First-year course work included history of Christian thought, liturgics, introduction to theology, and other foundational classes. But something essential was missing—a sense of the Spirit. The strong focus on developing the intellect gave short shrift to the formation and development of a mature spirituality, something I felt was a necessary and integral part of church leadership and the life of faith.

I struggled with various attitudes and approaches to people and life that I encountered in the seminary community. Only two weeks into academic year, a classmate began wearing a clerical collar and talked about "we," meaning the clergy (though we were seminarians and lay people), and "they," meaning others, or the laity. For him, the call to leadership mistakenly was taken as a call to separation, to power over, to elitism. Is this what seminary is about? I wondered.

Then there was integrative seminar. Initiated in previous years by students who sought to make an active connection between their academic work and their own spiritual journeys and questionings, integrative seminar had become a required course, complete with syllabus and rigid schedule. Burning questions were ignored or deferred until the scheduled, or appropriate, time. Once, when students were finally encouraged to voice their questions, a woman shared her confusion about the contrast she observed between what she thought the Bible said about homosexuality and her own experience of gay and lesbian people. The faculty facilitator quickly told her to wait until she took the pastoral care course, which would come a year or two later in the program.

I left the Master of Divinity program after that first year. My experience, while intellectually stimulating, was for the most part dry, spiritless, and frustrating. Clearly, I learned, the institutional church did not hold the corner on the spiritual market, and at times it stifled the movement of the Spirit instead of freeing it. More than anything, my seminary experience stirred my restlessness with the institutional church. After I left, I continued my spiritual quest more seriously than ever before, but

I also stopped attending church regularly. Something was missing in my experience of church. What was it? What was I looking for? What was faith really about?

My quest continued and new questions surfaced. Spiritual growth never occurs in a vacuum, and my own was nourished by everything from world events to friendships to books I read. About this time, I became more aware of the power and importance of systems and institutions—economic, political, judicial, religious, social—and how I was a part, active and de facto, of them. Startled by the statistic that Americans in the 1970s, while only six percent of the world's population, consumed forty percent of the world's resources, and encouraged and educated by others seeking to adopt a more "simple" lifestyle, I asked myself a new and uncomfortable question: How does my life affect the lives of others? I examined my own way of living and consuming in the light of faith, of "doing unto others," of being a good steward of the earth and its resources. What part did I play, knowingly and unknowingly, in depriving others of adequate food, clothing, shelter, medical care, or safe, fairly compensated work?

These were painful questions. I had always tried to be a good and honest person, not intentionally seeking to hurt or harm anyone or anything. Could I, even unwittingly, be a part of something evil? Could businesses, governments, industries, churches, and other societal institutions, while in the course of providing goods and services, enacting legislation, or supposedly serving God, be doing hurtful, harmful, and even evil things? These questions raised even more questions, not only about my personal lifestyle and things over which I felt I had some control but also about the society of which I was a part and about many things over which I felt I had little or no control. If I became convinced that certain governmental, business, or other actions were in direct (or even indirect) violation of the life of faith, how should I, how could I, respond? Like the testy lawyer in the parable of the good Samaritan, I too believed that a good neighbor is one who shows mercy to those who fall among robbers. But what did mercy involve, who were my neighbors, and who were the robbers?

I'd been raised to believe there were clear differentiations between good and evil, "good guys" and "bad guys." But the more I lived, the more complex and cloudy the issues of good and evil seemed to become. Even more confusing was the fact that people who vociferously claimed to know what was right and what was wrong often seemed to ignore the complexities and ambiguities of life as well as the gospel call to compassion. Tension grew between the admonition to "judge not" and the necessity to speak out against evil and to work for good. What does it mean, I kept asking in many different ways, for me to act lovingly, to act justly and mercifully?

Then the focus of my life questions shifted abruptly. As my first marriage failed, my questions about justice, mercy, and love focused on my closest and most intimate relationship: What does it mean to love? What does it mean to be loved? How do I love when I've been deeply hurt? Must one be able to trust in order to be able to love? Where do justice, mercy, and love meet in a broken relationship? As I went through the divorce, in sharp contrast to what I had been taught as a child, I now learned that I needed to put myself first sometimes. I had to begin to love and know myself before I could truly love and know others. I also needed to learn how to receive the love of others; I needed to learn how to be loved.

This movement inward led me back to graduate school—this time to the Graduate Theological Union (GTU) in Berkeley, California, where I focused my academic work on spirituality. I explored various forms and experiences of prayer, meditation, and other ways of developing the inner life. I found a spiritual director and met regularly to probe my spiritual questions and wrestlings. "How do I remain 'in God' at all times?" I asked. "Where is God leading me? How do I respond to God's call?"

The more deeply I moved into the inner life of the Spirit, the more I was drawn into the life of the world, though I still wrestled with how that should be expressed. I was writing on the spiritual crisis of divorce, leading workshops and retreats in spirituality, and doing some spiritual direction. But directly and indirectly I was encouraged, urged, and, at worst, harassed by members of the GTU community to become more active in social justice issues. Though I often supported positions taken on various issues, why didn't I engage in civil disobedience, picket weapons development laboratories, or block weapons shipments? Why didn't I express my faith as others did? Wasn't my faith active in response to the needs of the world? Wasn't I a "good" Christian, or was I just scared?

About this time, a local chapter of Pax Christi, a Roman Catholic peace group, sponsored a series of presentations on peacemaking. One of the speakers was Thomas Keating, a Trappist abbot, whose writing and speaking I admired. During a question and answer period, Keating was asked, "What is a peacemaker?" After a quick smile and a quip—"I'm sorry you asked that!"—to acknowledge the difficulty in adequately answering, Keating paused for a few moments. Then he responded, "A peacemaker is anyone who brings healing in this world." I breathed a sigh of relief. The work that I was doing in helping people to work through the pain of divorce or to develop a deeper spiritual life was a form of peacemaking too. Somehow I had known that, but when inundated by voices claiming that only certain expressions were truly peacemaking, I had begun to doubt that I was discerning God's call accurately.

But two or three people in the audience were not pleased with Keating's answer. They pressed him hard, asking if it weren't true that every Christian should be out on the picket lines demonstrating against weapons research and production. Keating stood his ground. He affirmed our need to be a prophetic voice and to call people of faith to be peacemakers. "But," he added, "we have no right to tell others how to express that. If," he went on, "a person is honestly following the leading of the Spirit, who are we to question the movement of the Spirit?"

Someone else's question, "What is a peacemaker?" brought new freedom to me. And Keating's emphasis on our need to be prophetic voices helped ground that freedom in faith. I realized I must continually ask myself how I am to express God's peace in my life each day. When I stop asking that question, when I stop listening for the different answers that are likely to emerge at different times in my life, my faith will have died. The inner and outer lives, at heart, are one. Each can help us live more faithfully, but we must enter fully into both for either to come to fruition.

⌘

Today the questions and questing of faith continue. Many of my earlier questions have resurfaced later in my life, spawning fresh expressions and explorations in the ever-changing environment of experience, circumstance, opportunity, and limits. Questions continually draw me into the spacious places of faith, often not without resistance, pain, or fear, but always with an undercurrent of graciousness.

As they have before, my questions and questing these days focus on seeking a balance between my inner and outer lives, between my work and the challenges of society, between my individual and communal faith journeys. Deeply convinced of and committed to the necessity of the Spirit being an integral part of human life, I constantly seek how the Spirit is moving today, not only in my life but in the lives of others as well. How do the old ways of faith inform contemporary experience? How does contemporary experience—particularly global awareness, cultural tensions and blendings, technological and scientific discoveries, environmental concerns—challenge and stretch traditional experiences, understandings, and expressions of faith?

During my years of study at the GTU, I discovered that I was part of the whole realm of faith, a realm that reached beyond the boundaries of my own denomination and even beyond the boundaries of Christianity. Narrow denominationalism faded as I discovered the strengths and weaknesses of various faith expressions within the Christian community and how much we needed one another. Beyond that I learned how the experiences of other faiths, of other spiritual seekings, could enhance, challenge, and revitalize my own heritage. The varied traditions of faith opened me to see the Spirit moving in ever new and surprising ways. In those years of study, exploration, and edge-pushing, I discovered that the riches and practical resources of the inner life ground, inform, and inspire, or breathe life into, the outward expressions of faith. Likewise the outward experiences challenge the inner life to stay rooted in reality, to be incarnate. Each continually asks: What does it mean to act in love here? Where is God present in this situation? What am I to give up or to give over to God here? How can I live more fully, more faithfully this day?

Yet the Spirit also moves in people who do not identify with any tradition. The Spirit, I am continually reminded, shows up in the most unlikely places—in a manger, on a cross, in the breaking of bread, among the outcasts of society. If only I, if only we, could expect to see the Spirit everywhere and in everyone. How would we treat our world, our neighbors near and far, all the creatures and wonders of the earth, if we really believed the Spirit permeates all of life?

In my neighborhood there is a popular bookstore devoted to the life of the spirit. Its ambiance is one of nurturance and care, beauty and peace. Sacred arts, books, and music of many traditions fill the store. Drums and rain sticks, beautifully crafted jewelry and smudge sticks mingle with crystals and compact discs. Gentle music plays in the background, while a pot with herbal tea waits to warm and calm weary souls. A huge basket sits near the front door with announcements of primal drumming workshops, shaman training, bodywork opportunities, women's rituals, and men's spirituality groups. Books, gathered neatly on beautifully handcrafted wooden tables and bookcases, offer guidance and inspiration ranging from recovery from addiction to healing the experience of childhood abuse, from meditation to poetry and fiction. Different approaches and orientations are offered, ranging from New Age, goddess worship, and Native

American traditions to representatives of the major world religions. The focus is one of seeking or rediscovering the Holy and the divine in ourselves and in the world around us, of connecting with the power that unites all.

What is striking about this bookstore and others like it is the dearth of Christian materials. Yet the spirit of this place is one of people seeking healing and life, not death. I find it very telling, that even in the world religions section, there are few representatives of Christianity. This dearth of Christian resources saddens me, because I do believe that the Christ-life still offers much to people today. But it also calls upon those of us whose roots lie in the Christian tradition to acknowledge our failure in communicating and sharing the life of the Spirit, our failure in loving.

Perhaps what it says more eloquently by its absence than its inclusion is that Christianity, in many of its manifestations, no longer speaks to the contemporary heart. The vision, the wisdom, the compassion, the justice, the possibility for human community that Christ taught and lived are often lost in the dogma, strictures, and structures of an institutional church set on preserving itself and of people seeking to justify the spiritual status quo, while others continue to hunger and thirst, both literally and figuratively.

The spiritual continuum precedes the Judeo-Christian tradition, precedes the "great" religions of the world. The human spirit has always sought, and I believe always will seek, some connection with the divine, the Holy, the matrix of all being. Perhaps rather than feeling threatened by others' experiences of the Holy, we might instead ask ourselves what we can learn from them.

But even as I am saddened by the perceived irrelevance of Christianity, I am also restless with Christianity myself. My spiritual roots run deep in the Christian tradition and it has given me life. But it has also stifled, stymied, and deeply wounded me through its often short-sighted human manifestations. Tradition can be stifling and stultifying, but it can also be life-giving. It can help reveal the path that many have traveled before. It can share hard-won wisdom and reveal ever-present questions, so we don't feel so alone in our search. Sometimes, if in no other way, tradition serves as a starting point for further spiritual exploration, the personal spiritual journey that each of us makes alone.

I seek a way to embrace the riches of tradition without its excesses, blindnesses, and prejudices. I wrestle with my relationship with the church as a whole and with the denomination that spawned me. I worship communally, but my primary spiritual sustenance comes from my own daily spiritual practice and informal but frequent sharing with other seekers on the way. For years I went to church because I had to or because I felt I should. But I can and will no longer do that. If church does not nurture me and challenge me to grow in the Spirit and in truth, I will not go simply for the sake of being a "faithful church-goer," because being a faithful church-goer and being faithful are not necessarily synonymous.

Yet one of my greatest temptations is to seek the world of faith wholly on my own. I need to seek faith alone, but I need also to seek it communally. I need to constantly guard against my own complacency and rationalizations about how I am to be a person of faith. Am I rationalizing when I maintain that I often find deeper spiritual sustenance in an hour of silent meditation than an hour of Sunday morning communal worship? Maybe yes, maybe no. Am I avoiding the ongoing challenges of putting love into action in the church, often one of the most daunting places to do that? Are there some who "belong" in the institutional church, for whom the church animates and cultivates their faith and the living out of their faith in the world? I believe, and know, there are many faithful, seriously seeking, and spiritually wise people who remain active in the institutional church; they are its life-blood and our hope. Are there others who "belong" outside the institutional church, who are more fully faithful in the community of the world? Are there times, in order for spiritual growth to proceed most fully, for people of faith to be "in" the institutional church and other times for them to be "out"? Are there times when we would grow more fully if we felt the freedom to move from one denomination or faith to another, to glean from those different traditions the riches, the style, the focus that we most need for growth at a particular time in our lives?

And yet I continue to long for a community of faith of which I can be a part with openness and integrity, a community that will nurture me, nourish me, challenge me, guide me. I long for a community that will offer me both deep, healthy roots and strong, resilient wings with which to fly. I hope for a community with patience and certainty of spirit that allows it to face and encounter the complexity and ambiguity of our world. I long for a community that is compassionate and wise in facing and struggling with the gray areas of life—the places where life and death are not clearly delineated, where good and evil seem inextricably bound, where the past is troubled, the present complex, the future uncertain. I have such a community in dispersion, friends and fellow seekers spread across the States and throughout the world. Yet I seek a proximate community as well. I seek all these things, because I yearn for a world that is compassionate and wise, and because I believe that the community of faith can be a leaven of compassion and wisdom in the world.

But just as the church or the community of faith can and should be a catalyst to living the Christ-life in the world, of leavening wisdom and compassion, so it can also be a hideaway, a clique, a self-justifying bastion against the often harsh and difficult challenges of living as people of faith fully engaged in and with the world. It can be a way of avoiding the raw and often lonely personal spiritual quest that we can only do on our own. But remaining outside the church can operate in the same way. We all—"inside" or "outside," "active" or "inactive," "churched" or "unchurched"—can fall into the trap of crying "Lord, Lord" and then, dumbfounded, realize we haven't been living a faithful life at all.

Yet, in the midst of the complexity and confusion of all these questions and issues, in the midst of my own uncertainty, shortcomings, and shortsightedness, I keep trying, in faith, to discern, to seek, and to choose life over death. This is what I must do, and it is all that I can do.

⚬

We are, I believe, at a crucial time in our world in many ways, including the way of faith. We waver on the edge of the emergence of a new understanding of ourselves, our world, and our God. We teeter between destroying ourselves and life as we know it, or laboring into the rough and raw birthing of something we as yet can at most barely imagine. And as that new life struggles into being, we struggle too—we struggle to understand, to comprehend, to conceive of something that is different from the ways of thinking and being and believing that we have regarded normative or sacred. At this exciting, fateful time, some attempt to throw out the past altogether; others cling almost violently to it, eschewing any and all change as evil, anti-God, and anti-Christ. Somehow we need to retain what is valuable from the past and move with courage and vigor into the future, while remaining vibrantly alive and willing to question, to struggle, and to work in the only time we really have: *Now*.

Our questions can serve us well in a time such as this, a time of grave uncertainty, of soaring potential, of fragile yet resilient hope. Our questions and questing are crucial, because they can help us live into the answer of the future. I am certain of one thing: the love that is God is at the heart of the answer, just as it is at the heart of each moment—past, present, and future. Faith today, tomorrow, and always seeks to live, to love, and to be loved fully. It seeks the Holy and waits (though not always patiently) to be found; it nurtures and activates wisdom and compassion. It chooses to embrace hope and to be embraced by hope, even when overwhelmed by despair; it seeks life even in the face of death. We act in faith, knowing that we see only dimly.

But living in faith, we act anyway, choosing and doing the best we can. We act and live in confidence that someday we will see face to face, that we will live into the answers. For God's grace embraces our questions as well as our answers and our blindness as well as our vision, just as the sun shines steadily through the night, waiting to illumine the sky at dawn. ෬

ରେ

Epilogue

ᬝ

Many times over the years, the story of Jacob has encouraged me. I return to it when I am weary or frightened, for Jacob was weary and frightened too. I tell myself that if Jacob could wrestle when he was tired and scared, perhaps I can do the same. If Jacob could wrest a blessing from the one with whom he wrestles, perhaps I can too. If Jacob could see the face of God in his struggle, if even in his pain he could recognize God, if he could walk into the light of dawn with his limp as a reminder not of defeat but of confidence in the steadfast Holy Presence, then perhaps I can as well. I wish the same for you. ᬝ

NOTES

CHAPTER FOUR

1. Systemic lupus erythematosus, a rather bizarre and sometimes baffling disease, disrupts the body's immune system. Antibodies and lymphocytes (cells that ordinarily fight infections) proliferate and turn against the body's own cells, causing a variety of disorders including high fever, arthritic-like joint pain, and possible damage to the kidneys, blood, heart, lungs, skin, or central nervous system. It is often accompanied by a distinctive facial rash, once thought to be the result of a wolf bite, hence the name *lupus* (Latin, wolf). The cause of the disease, whose most frequent victims are women of child-bearing age, is unknown and there is no known cure.

2. Elizabeth O'Connor, "Learnings from an Illness," *Cry Pain, Cry Hope* (Waco, TX: Word Books, 1987), 114.

3. The actual quote is: "Healing is a creative act, calling for all the hard work and dedication needed for other forms of creativity." Bernie S. Siegel, M.D., *Love, Medicine & Miracles* (New York: Harper & Row, 1986), 41.

CHAPTER FIVE

1. Cited in the August 1991 newsletter of the *Ministry of Money* (Gaithersburg, MD), 3-40. My reflections on the stories of the rich young man and Zacchaeus grow out of the insights of John Haughey, contained in this newsletter.

2. Quoted in Howard Moody, "The Meanings of Money," *Christianity and Crisis* 51 (June 10, 1991), 189.

CHAPTER SIX

1. Quoted in May Sarton, *After the Stroke: A Journal* (New York: W. W. Norton & Company, 1988), 259.

CHAPTER SEVEN

1. John Francis Kavanaugh, *Following Christ in a Consumer Society: The Spirituality of Cultural Resistance* (Maryknoll, NY: Orbis Books, 1981), 99.

CHAPTER EIGHT

1. Rainer Maria Rilke, *Letters to a Young Poet,* trans. M. D. Herter Norton (New York: W. W. Norton, 1954), 35.

ABOUT THE AUTHOR

cx

Jean M. Blomquist lives and writes in Berkeley, California. She received her undergraduate degree in English from California Lutheran College in Thousand Oaks, California, and her graduate degree in the History and Phenomenology of Religions from The Graduate Theological Union in Berkeley, California.

The author is a frequent contributor to *Weavings: A Journal of the Christian Spiritual Life* and has had articles published in *Pastoral Psychology, The Lutheran, Lutheran Women,* and *The Upper Room Disciplines.* She also lectures and leads workshops and retreats on the spiritual life.

She enjoys reading, gardening, hiking, cooking, calligraphy, and music. She is married to Gregory Kepferle.

Photo by Claudia Marseille